RADIUS: Network Control and Authentication

James Relington

DEDICATION

To those who seek knowledge, inspiration, and new perspectives—
may this book be a companion on your journey, a spark for curiosity,
and a reminder that every page turned is a step toward discovery.

AKNOWLEDGEMENTS

I would like to express my deepest gratitude to everyone who contributed to the creation of this book. To my colleagues and mentors, your insights and expertise have been invaluable. A special thank you to my family and friends for their unwavering support and encouragement throughout this journey.

Introduction to RADIUS

Remote Authentication Dial-In User Service, commonly known as RADIUS, represents one of the fundamental pillars of modern network security and control. Developed originally in the early 1990s, this protocol quickly evolved into an essential mechanism for managing access and authentication within diverse network environments. RADIUS became particularly prominent due to its straightforward yet powerful approach, providing centralized authentication, authorization, and accounting for users attempting to gain access to networks and networked services. Its continued popularity can be attributed to its flexibility and broad support across various types of network equipment, software systems, and authentication methods.

RADIUS operates by positioning a centralized authentication server within a network environment, thus allowing administrators to effectively manage and secure access without requiring complex or repetitive configurations on every network access device. When a user attempts to connect to a network resource, such as through a wireless access point, VPN gateway, or switch port, their credentials and connection information are encapsulated into a RADIUS packet and forwarded from the Network Access Server to the RADIUS server. The RADIUS server then evaluates these credentials against its stored database, which may include local user accounts, LDAP directories, Active Directory, or external SQL databases. After validating the user's identity, the server returns an accept or reject response, alongside necessary configuration attributes that dictate the permissions and parameters of the user's session.

One reason for the widespread adoption of RADIUS is its simplicity. Despite its minimalistic and efficient packet structure, RADIUS can convey a considerable amount of information through the use of Attribute-Value Pairs (AVPs). These attributes allow administrators to pass detailed instructions, such as VLAN assignments, access restrictions, session time limits, and various authorization rules, directly from the authentication server to network devices. Thus, network administrators can enforce consistent security policies across numerous entry points and devices, significantly simplifying network management tasks.

Another compelling aspect of RADIUS is its inherent versatility. It supports a broad spectrum of authentication protocols, from basic methods such as Password Authentication Protocol (PAP) and Challenge Handshake Authentication Protocol (CHAP) to more advanced mechanisms, including Extensible Authentication Protocol (EAP). This versatility empowers network administrators to adapt their security infrastructure according to their unique organizational needs, security requirements, and user scenarios. Moreover, RADIUS seamlessly integrates with IEEE 802.1X, providing robust authentication capabilities for both wired and wireless network environments, thus ensuring comprehensive coverage for virtually all potential network entry points.

Beyond mere authentication, RADIUS also handles essential accounting functions, meticulously tracking and logging user session activities for auditing and compliance purposes. Each RADIUS accounting request records information regarding session duration, data usage, connection timestamps, and specific actions performed by users during their network sessions. This granular accounting capability makes RADIUS invaluable in scenarios requiring detailed accountability, such as in ISP billing environments or enterprise networks subject to strict regulatory oversight. By maintaining accurate and centralized records, administrators can easily generate detailed reports, monitor usage patterns, identify suspicious activities, and swiftly respond to any potential security incidents.

Security remains one of the foremost concerns of contemporary network infrastructure, and RADIUS addresses this effectively through several measures. Although originally developed for use over insecure network connections, modern implementations of RADIUS increasingly utilize robust encryption methods to protect sensitive user authentication data. Protocols such as IPsec tunnels or Transport Layer Security (TLS) have become standard practice in securing RADIUS traffic, ensuring that authentication credentials remain confidential and resistant to interception or replay attacks. Furthermore, using dedicated RADIUS servers allows administrators to isolate critical security processes, limiting exposure to potential vulnerabilities.

The practicality and scalability of RADIUS are particularly evident in large-scale deployments, where hundreds or even thousands of network access points require consistent authentication and authorization mechanisms. In such complex scenarios, the centralized nature of RADIUS streamlines administrative tasks significantly. Network managers can implement global policy changes, update user permissions, or modify authentication procedures rapidly and uniformly, without needing individual adjustments across disparate systems. Additionally, RADIUS inherently supports hierarchical deployments, redundancy, and load balancing, enabling robust configurations capable of handling intensive authentication loads while maintaining high availability and performance.

Although RADIUS continues to evolve, with newer protocols such as Diameter attempting to replace or complement its functionality, it remains an essential element within the landscape of network security due to its reliability, interoperability, and widespread acceptance among vendors and enterprises alike. Its sustained relevance underscores the strength and practicality of its original design, reinforcing why network engineers and administrators worldwide continue to rely heavily on RADIUS as the backbone for authentication and access control within increasingly interconnected environments. RADIUS is not only fundamental to secure network access; it embodies the broader shift toward centralized, controlled, and accountable network management practices in today's digitally driven world.

Evolution of Network Authentication

The evolution of network authentication has closely mirrored the growth and increasing complexity of network technologies themselves, evolving from simplistic, trust-based methods to highly sophisticated, cryptographic protocols designed to withstand modern security threats. At the dawn of networked computing, authentication was practically nonexistent. Early networks, often confined to single laboratories or organizations, relied on simple trust relationships. Physical proximity and limited access to computing hardware meant security was rarely a serious concern. Authentication, when it occurred at all, typically took the form of simple passwords or personal recognition among a small, closely connected user group.

As networking expanded beyond localized environments, initially through dial-up connections and later through more extensive networks such as the Internet, the need for robust authentication became evident. Password-based authentication quickly became the dominant approach due to its simplicity and ease of deployment. However, passwords introduced multiple vulnerabilities, particularly when transmitted in clear text across unsecured channels. Early protocols such as Telnet and FTP, for instance, transmitted authentication data without encryption, making them susceptible to interception and eavesdropping. The widespread adoption of password-based methods without additional security measures proved increasingly inadequate, prompting a wave of innovations and improvements in authentication strategies.

The rise of remote-access networking in the late 1980s and early 1990s marked a significant shift toward stronger, more reliable authentication methods. Protocols like Password Authentication Protocol (PAP) and Challenge Handshake Authentication Protocol

(CHAP) emerged as early attempts to address vulnerabilities inherent in transmitting credentials over unsecured networks. PAP, despite being an improvement over entirely unprotected password transmissions, still sent passwords in clear text, leaving it vulnerable. CHAP offered more substantial improvements by employing challenge-response mechanisms, where passwords were never directly sent across the network. Instead, cryptographic hashes validated the user's knowledge of the correct password, providing protection against casual interception. Although these methods represented significant progress, network threats continued evolving, creating a demand for even more secure and versatile authentication frameworks.

By the mid-1990s, organizations required centralized, scalable authentication solutions capable of handling the rapid expansion of remote access services, such as dial-up internet connections, Virtual Private Networks (VPNs), and wireless connectivity. In response to this need, protocols such as RADIUS emerged, providing centralized authentication, authorization, and accounting. RADIUS revolutionized network management by enabling administrators to control authentication across diverse network access points from a single server, significantly enhancing security, efficiency, and manageability. Its adoption rapidly spread among enterprises and Internet Service Providers (ISPs), becoming the standard for centralized authentication due to its compatibility, flexibility, and ease of use.

Alongside centralized systems like RADIUS, the late 1990s and early 2000s brought additional advancements driven by the expanding landscape of wireless networks and the broader proliferation of mobile and portable devices. This era saw the development and standardization of IEEE 802.1X, which offered a structured framework for secure network access control. IEEE 802.1X integrated seamlessly with authentication protocols such as RADIUS and Extensible Authentication Protocol (EAP), providing rigorous authentication at the network port or wireless access point. This significantly improved the security of both wired and wireless networks, preventing unauthorized devices from gaining network access and allowing granular control over user permissions and device access policies.

Moreover, Extensible Authentication Protocol (EAP) played a crucial role in the evolution of network authentication by enabling greater flexibility and modularity. EAP became an essential foundation for implementing various secure authentication methods, such as EAP-TLS, EAP-TTLS, and PEAP, which integrated certificate-based authentication and mutual authentication techniques. These advanced EAP methods offered vastly improved security by ensuring the identities of both client and server, reducing vulnerability to man-in-the-middle and spoofing attacks. This integration represented a significant evolution in authentication methodology, transitioning from mere passwords to cryptographic, certificate-based identity management and robust mutual authentication mechanisms.

Authentication methods continued to evolve rapidly, driven by increasing threats from cyber-attacks, growing demands for mobility and flexibility, and evolving regulatory compliance requirements. Multi-factor authentication (MFA) emerged as an essential evolution in securing networks, combining something a user knows, such as a password, with something they have, like a physical token or smartphone, or something they are, such as biometric data. The adoption of MFA greatly increased network security, significantly mitigating the risks associated with compromised passwords. Its implementation became widespread in critical applications, sensitive corporate environments, and increasingly among everyday users, reflecting a broader societal shift towards stronger and multi-layered authentication practices.

Today, the trajectory of network authentication continues toward greater sophistication, incorporating biometrics, context-aware security, adaptive authentication mechanisms, and artificial intelligence-driven threat detection. Modern authentication systems integrate seamlessly with cloud-based environments, federated identity management solutions, and single sign-on (SSO) architectures, ensuring comprehensive security across complex, distributed systems. Network authentication now extends beyond mere user verification, encompassing detailed user behavior analytics, dynamic risk assessment, and real-time response to security events, reflecting an increasingly nuanced understanding of network security dynamics.

As networked technologies continue to proliferate, expanding into virtually every aspect of modern life, authentication methods will inevitably become even more advanced and diverse, adapting continuously to combat emerging threats and support expanding technological capabilities. Authentication will persist as an essential, ever-evolving component of secure and efficient network access, reflecting the complexity and interconnectedness of the digital age.

Understanding Authentication Protocols

Authentication protocols constitute the foundation of secure communication within networked environments, playing a crucial role in verifying identities and granting appropriate access to resources. At their core, authentication protocols provide structured methods for exchanging credentials securely between users or devices and authentication servers. Such protocols are essential in protecting network infrastructure from unauthorized access, identity theft, and various cyber threats. A comprehensive understanding of authentication protocols is vital for network administrators, cybersecurity professionals, and technology architects tasked with protecting sensitive information and ensuring network integrity.

Initially, authentication protocols relied heavily on simplistic mechanisms such as transmitting clear-text passwords over networks. While straightforward and easy to implement, these early methods exposed organizations to severe vulnerabilities, such as interception and credential theft. As network environments expanded and threats grew more sophisticated, secure authentication protocols evolved significantly, integrating stronger cryptographic techniques, mutual verification, and challenge-response mechanisms to enhance security. This evolution highlights an ongoing effort to balance user convenience with robust security requirements, driving continual innovation in authentication methodologies.

Password Authentication Protocol (PAP) represents one of the earliest examples of authentication protocols and offers a clear illustration of basic functionality combined with significant security limitations. Under PAP, users submit credentials in plain text to the authentication server, which then verifies them against a stored database. Due to the absence of encryption or hashing, PAP remains highly vulnerable to interception by unauthorized individuals, particularly in environments lacking secure communication channels. Despite these limitations, PAP historically served as an essential stepping-stone, prompting the development of improved protocols that addressed its inherent weaknesses.

Responding to PAP's security gaps, protocols like Challenge Handshake Authentication Protocol (CHAP) introduced significant improvements by incorporating a challenge-response method. CHAP avoids sending passwords directly over the network; instead, the authentication server issues a random challenge to the connecting client, which combines it with a secret key or password to generate a cryptographic hash response. The server independently computes the expected response, verifying identity without exposing sensitive information directly. This method significantly mitigates risks associated with credential theft, replay attacks, and interception, marking a major milestone in authentication protocol advancement.

The subsequent emergence of Extensible Authentication Protocol (EAP) transformed the landscape of authentication protocols, offering increased versatility, scalability, and security. EAP, originally designed as a generic authentication framework, supports various authentication methods within a standardized negotiation process, providing extensive flexibility for integrating emerging technologies and evolving authentication needs. By serving as a container for different authentication mechanisms, EAP enables network administrators to select appropriate authentication techniques based on organizational policies, threat models, and network infrastructure requirements.

Advanced EAP methods, such as EAP-TLS, EAP-TTLS, and Protected EAP (PEAP), offer robust and secure authentication approaches by employing digital certificates, encrypted tunnels, and mutual authentication. For instance, EAP-TLS provides mutual authentication by requiring both client and server certificates, ensuring that both parties validate each other's identity before communication begins. While delivering superior security, EAP-TLS implementation can be complex due to requirements for managing public key infrastructures

(PKI). PEAP and EAP-TTLS simplify deployment by using secure tunnels to encapsulate user credentials, protecting authentication exchanges without necessarily requiring client-side certificates. These advanced protocols are widely deployed in secure wireless and wired networks, enterprise environments, and public institutions demanding high-security authentication.

IEEE 802.1X further illustrates the practical application of authentication protocols within contemporary networking environments. Commonly integrated with EAP and RADIUS, IEEE 802.1X provides port-based network access control, effectively ensuring that network resources remain protected until client authentication succeeds. In this scenario, authentication protocols are essential in maintaining the secure boundary between trusted and untrusted devices. This integration allows network administrators to centrally manage policies, permissions, and access privileges, significantly enhancing overall network security and administrative control.

Beyond password-based or certificate-based authentication protocols, token-based authentication mechanisms have gained traction due to their strong security properties. Protocols utilizing time-based or event-based tokens, often generated by hardware or software authenticators, provide robust two-factor authentication methods. These tokens generate dynamic credentials, valid only briefly, substantially reducing the risk associated with stolen or compromised passwords. Such token-based protocols offer critical security enhancements, particularly when combined with other authentication methods, creating layered security that significantly complicates unauthorized access attempts.

Modern authentication protocols increasingly incorporate adaptive and context-aware approaches, analyzing user behavior, device status, geographical location, and real-time risk assessments to dynamically determine authentication requirements. Adaptive authentication protocols offer substantial security improvements by tailoring authentication demands based on perceived risk levels. For example, unusual user behavior or connection attempts from unexpected locations may trigger additional verification steps, such as multi-factor authentication, biometric validation, or behavioral analytics, effectively responding to evolving threats.

Authentication protocols continue adapting to emerging technological paradigms such as cloud computing, mobile platforms, IoT devices, and federated identity systems. Protocols like OAuth, OpenID Connect, and SAML facilitate seamless authentication across multiple services, allowing users to authenticate once and securely access multiple resources or applications. Federated authentication protocols simplify user experiences while maintaining rigorous security standards, enabling efficient interoperability across organizational boundaries.

The sustained evolution of authentication protocols highlights a perpetual need to respond proactively to emerging cybersecurity threats and the rapid proliferation of connected devices. Network administrators, security professionals, and IT strategists must maintain awareness of authentication protocol advancements, understanding their practical implications and potential limitations within diverse operational contexts. Robust, carefully implemented authentication protocols remain indispensable in maintaining secure, trustworthy network environments capable of defending sensitive data against increasingly sophisticated threats.

RADIUS Architecture Overview

The Remote Authentication Dial-In User Service architecture, more commonly known as RADIUS, is constructed around the core concept of centralized management of authentication, authorization, and accounting services within networked environments. Designed initially to simplify the administration of dial-in modem pools, RADIUS evolved rapidly into a versatile protocol, adaptable to various networking technologies such as wired Ethernet connections, Wi-Fi networks, and Virtual Private Networks. The foundational architecture of RADIUS centers around the interaction between three essential components: the client or Network Access Server (NAS), the centralized RADIUS server itself, and an associated database that stores user credentials and policy information. Together, these components create a seamless and robust system capable of securely managing user access at scale.

At the heart of the RADIUS architecture lies the central RADIUS server, typically hosted on dedicated infrastructure designed for security and scalability. This server acts as the primary authority responsible for processing authentication requests and determining appropriate user permissions. When a user attempts network access—through a VPN gateway, wireless access point, or Ethernet switch port—the NAS receives the initial connection attempt. Rather than performing authentication locally, the NAS delegates this task to the centralized RADIUS server, transmitting user-supplied credentials within a standardized RADIUS authentication request packet. The RADIUS server, upon receiving this request, evaluates the credentials against stored records. Depending upon the outcome of this evaluation, the server sends back a response packet instructing the NAS whether to accept or deny network access to the user.

The client component, commonly referred to as the NAS, serves as the intermediary between end-users and the centralized RADIUS server. It plays a pivotal role by translating initial connection attempts into properly formatted RADIUS packets and managing the subsequent authentication responses from the RADIUS server. NAS devices are typically specialized network equipment, such as routers, switches, VPN concentrators, or wireless access points. The critical advantage of utilizing NAS devices within the RADIUS architecture is the significant reduction in administrative overhead. Rather than requiring each device to maintain extensive local user databases, authentication and authorization decisions are centralized, thereby simplifying configuration, reducing inconsistencies, and enhancing network security through uniform policy enforcement.

Integral to the RADIUS architecture is the database component, which houses user credentials, access policies, and accounting data. This backend database may be a simple flat-file storage system or a sophisticated relational database like SQL or LDAP-based directories, including Microsoft Active Directory. RADIUS servers can query these databases dynamically, validating user identities, determining allowed network resources, and retrieving detailed policy instructions for the NAS to enforce. By abstracting user data storage away from NAS devices and centralizing it within a single database or directory service, the RADIUS architecture achieves greater scalability and flexibility, essential in large enterprises, Internet service providers, and complex multi-site networks.

The communication between NAS devices and RADIUS servers occurs via standardized RADIUS packets, characterized by their compact and efficient format. These packets encapsulate necessary information, including user credentials, access attributes, session identifiers, and other critical control data, structured in Attribute-Value Pairs (AVPs). The use of AVPs enables RADIUS servers to pass highly detailed configuration instructions to NAS devices, including IP address assignments, VLAN tagging information, session duration limits, and access privileges. This design not only simplifies the implementation of sophisticated authorization schemes but also ensures compatibility and interoperability across diverse networking equipment from multiple vendors.

In addition to authentication and authorization, the RADIUS architecture provides a powerful and detailed accounting capability. Accounting records are systematically generated and stored to document user activities during network sessions, providing comprehensive tracking and auditing data for network administrators. These accounting packets, transmitted separately from authentication and authorization exchanges, contain detailed session logs, usage statistics, connection timestamps, and other relevant data. By maintaining accurate, centralized accounting records, RADIUS servers allow administrators to analyze network usage patterns, enforce compliance policies, optimize resource allocation, and identify security threats or misuse promptly.

The flexibility inherent in the RADIUS architecture also allows for hierarchical or proxy-based implementations, particularly valuable for large networks spanning geographic locations or organizational units. RADIUS proxy servers enable forwarding authentication requests to specialized or remote RADIUS servers based on predefined rules or attribute criteria. This arrangement facilitates decentralized management while preserving centralized control and consistent policy enforcement, thereby enhancing scalability, redundancy, and overall reliability of the network authentication infrastructure.

Security considerations within RADIUS architecture include ensuring confidentiality, integrity, and availability of communications between NAS devices and servers. While traditional implementations of RADIUS relied on simple shared secrets for basic packet authentication, modern environments increasingly adopt additional security layers such as IPsec tunnels or Transport Layer Security (TLS) to protect sensitive authentication information in transit. Encrypting RADIUS exchanges effectively mitigates risks from interception or tampering, particularly essential in public, wireless, or distributed network deployments.

RADIUS architecture continues to prove itself as a robust, scalable, and adaptable framework for centralized network control, capable of accommodating the constantly evolving security requirements of modern networking environments. Its simplicity, combined with extensive flexibility and interoperability, explains its widespread adoption across numerous industries and technological contexts. As enterprises, ISPs, and organizations face increasingly complex security demands and expand network infrastructure, the foundational principles of RADIUS architecture remain critically important in maintaining secure, reliable, and efficient user authentication and management services.

RADIUS Packet Structure

The RADIUS packet structure serves as the fundamental building block through which Remote Authentication Dial-In User Service exchanges essential information between Network Access Servers (NAS) and RADIUS authentication servers. Understanding the detailed composition and functionality of RADIUS packets is crucial for network administrators and cybersecurity specialists, as these packets carry all necessary authentication, authorization, and accounting data across the network. Each RADIUS packet follows a carefully defined format, designed to ensure compatibility, efficiency, and reliability in various networking environments, from small businesses to global enterprises and ISPs.

A typical RADIUS packet consists of four distinct elements: a fixed-size header, an authenticator field, a series of Attribute-Value Pairs (AVPs), and padding for alignment if necessary. The fixed header is precisely twenty bytes long, containing essential information needed by receiving systems to correctly interpret and process the incoming packet. This header includes key fields such as the packet type, packet identifier, and packet length. The packet type indicates the nature of the RADIUS message—whether it is an authentication request, authentication accept, authentication reject, or accounting message— allowing immediate recognition of the packet's purpose by the receiving device. Properly understanding these packet types ensures efficient troubleshooting, accurate network diagnostics, and effective management of user sessions.

The packet identifier, another essential header component, consists of a single-byte numeric value that uniquely associates requests with their corresponding responses. This mechanism is vital in environments with heavy traffic loads, as it allows NAS devices and RADIUS servers to match responses accurately to their originating requests, even when multiple simultaneous authentication processes are occurring. Furthermore, packet length, also stored within the header, specifies the total length of the packet, including both header and all Attribute-Value Pairs, enabling accurate extraction and decoding of data at the receiving end.

Following the header is the authenticator field, a sixteen-byte value whose purpose varies depending on packet type. In an Access-Request packet, for instance, this field contains a randomly generated value called the request authenticator. This value plays a crucial role in securing communication by providing a basis for encrypting user passwords, thus protecting sensitive credential data against interception or unauthorized disclosure. Conversely, in response packets such as Access-Accept or Access-Reject, this authenticator is calculated from a hash of the packet contents combined with a shared secret key known only to the NAS and the RADIUS server. Such cryptographic validation ensures packet integrity, safeguarding against manipulation, replay attacks, and spoofing attempts.

Perhaps the most flexible and extensively utilized component within the RADIUS packet is the collection of Attribute-Value Pairs. Each AVP represents specific information relevant to the authentication or authorization process, stored as discrete pairs consisting of an attribute identifier, a length field, and the associated attribute value. The AVP structure provides remarkable flexibility, allowing packets to convey detailed user credentials, authentication methods, session parameters, and other relevant control data to the RADIUS server. For example, AVPs can specify items such as username, encrypted passwords, network access privileges, session time limits, VLAN assignments, IP address allocation, and specific instructions on handling the user's connection request. This structure ensures consistent and efficient enforcement of organizational policies and security rules across all access points.

The extensible design of AVPs allows vendors to define their own proprietary attributes, known as Vendor-Specific Attributes (VSAs). VSAs enable vendors to integrate unique or specialized features into RADIUS implementations while preserving interoperability. This extensibility ensures that the RADIUS packet structure can continually adapt and evolve in response to emerging network technologies, business requirements, and security challenges. While VSAs increase complexity slightly, their presence significantly enhances the versatility and practical applicability of RADIUS across diverse networking contexts and equipment manufacturers.

The encoding of sensitive AVPs, particularly passwords, exemplifies the importance of robust encryption within the RADIUS packet structure. RADIUS employs a specialized method for password encryption, using the request authenticator and a shared secret to produce an encrypted representation of user passwords. This encrypted form prevents clear-text passwords from being transmitted over the network, considerably enhancing security during authentication exchanges. Accurate encryption and decryption processes, dependent on the correct packet structure and shared secrets, are critical to maintaining the confidentiality and integrity of authentication data.

While transmitting accounting information, RADIUS packets adhere to a similar structure, yet their AVPs focus heavily on session data, including session duration, bytes transferred, timestamps, and user activities. Accounting packets use specific packet types—Accounting-

Request and Accounting-Response—to distinguish them from authentication transactions. Maintaining detailed and standardized accounting packets allows administrators to perform accurate auditing, resource tracking, and compliance monitoring, crucial in regulated environments or usage-based billing scenarios.

The RADIUS packet structure, though compact and straightforward, encompasses complex interactions involving precise definitions and strict compliance with the protocol standard. Misinterpretation, improper formatting, or inconsistent use of fields can lead to authentication failures, degraded security, or interoperability issues. Thus, network engineers and security professionals must develop comprehensive familiarity with the intricacies of RADIUS packets, ensuring their deployments comply fully with the protocol's stringent specifications and best practices. Mastery of this packet structure directly contributes to maintaining robust, secure, and reliable authentication services across contemporary network environments.

Attribute-Value Pairs (AVPs)

Attribute-Value Pairs (AVPs) represent a critical and highly versatile element of the Remote Authentication Dial-In User Service (RADIUS) protocol, providing a structured means for encoding essential data within RADIUS packets. These pairs form the primary method by which information related to user authentication, authorization decisions, and accounting data is exchanged between Network Access Servers (NAS) and RADIUS servers. AVPs deliver significant flexibility to RADIUS implementations, enabling the protocol to handle diverse network environments, support multiple authentication mechanisms, and dynamically convey detailed configuration information across distributed network infrastructure.

Each Attribute-Value Pair within a RADIUS packet comprises three essential components: an attribute type identifier, a length indicator, and the actual value associated with that attribute. The attribute type is defined numerically, specifying precisely the nature of the information contained within the pair. For instance, attributes can identify a user's username, password, assigned IP address, session timeout duration, VLAN identifier, or access privileges. The length indicator explicitly marks the total size of the AVP, including the attribute type, length byte, and value itself, ensuring accurate parsing by the receiving RADIUS server or NAS device. The attribute value component holds the actual data content, formatted according to the attribute type's predefined structure and meaning, ensuring consistency and interoperability across various vendor implementations.

RADIUS attributes are standardized and regulated to ensure that all RADIUS-compatible equipment and software can correctly interpret and process them. Initially, the Internet Assigned Numbers Authority (IANA) reserved a finite range of numerical identifiers to represent specific standard attributes, establishing a well-defined and universally understood vocabulary. Among these standard attributes are fundamental identifiers such as User-Name, User-Password, NAS-IP-Address, NAS-Identifier, Session-Timeout, and Framed-IP-Address. These standard attributes significantly simplify interoperability and provide the baseline for RADIUS implementations across diverse networking scenarios.

The power and flexibility of AVPs arise from the extensibility built into the RADIUS protocol itself, allowing vendors and organizations to define additional attributes beyond the standard set. Known as Vendor-Specific Attributes (VSAs), these specialized AVPs provide the means to encode proprietary data or vendor-specific functionality within RADIUS communications. Vendors assign unique numerical identifiers within an IANA-reserved range, embedding data that is relevant specifically to their network equipment or software systems. VSAs are critical to accommodating diverse operational requirements or innovative features that standard attributes do not adequately address. Network administrators, therefore, gain increased control and customization options when integrating RADIUS with unique organizational needs or specialized network hardware.

A particularly valuable use of AVPs is seen in authentication and authorization decisions. Upon successful authentication, the RADIUS server communicates authorization parameters back to the NAS device through AVPs, specifying precisely what resources and privileges the authenticated user should receive. This may include information such as which VLAN the user should join, how long their network session may last, the IP address assigned to their connection, and bandwidth restrictions. Consequently, the flexibility and expressiveness of AVPs facilitate detailed and granular policy enforcement. By encoding such information directly into AVPs, network administrators ensure uniform application of authorization policies across all network entry points, streamlining administration and significantly improving network security posture.

The dynamic nature of AVPs also supports advanced authentication scenarios and complex session management requirements. Advanced authentication protocols such as Extensible Authentication Protocol (EAP) rely heavily on AVPs to communicate parameters, results, and session details throughout the authentication exchange. EAP-specific attributes encapsulate essential data, such as authentication types, client responses, and cryptographic exchanges, enabling sophisticated authentication mechanisms such as mutual authentication and certificate-based validation. Without AVPs, achieving such advanced authentication processes within RADIUS would be exceedingly difficult or even impractical, highlighting the importance of their structured flexibility and universal applicability.

Encryption and security considerations play a crucial role in the handling of sensitive AVPs, particularly user passwords or cryptographic keys transmitted between NAS devices and RADIUS servers. RADIUS employs a secure method of encrypting sensitive attribute values, relying on a shared secret key between the communicating parties. The encryption ensures confidentiality during transmission, preventing the exposure of critical authentication data. AVPs containing sensitive information like passwords thus maintain robust protection against interception or unauthorized access attempts, underscoring the critical importance of implementing secure key management practices and secure communication channels within RADIUS deployments.

Moreover, the extensibility of AVPs extends naturally to the accounting capabilities of RADIUS, where detailed information about user sessions, resource usage, and connection history are captured and transmitted using AVPs designed explicitly for accounting purposes. Accounting AVPs encompass session identifiers, timestamps, session durations, byte counters for data transferred, and specific user actions recorded during network access periods. By capturing detailed and accurate accounting records, AVPs enable network administrators and service providers to conduct thorough usage analyses, monitor compliance with regulatory requirements, implement accurate billing procedures, and detect anomalous behaviors indicative of security threats or policy violations.

The simplicity, efficiency, and adaptability inherent in the AVP design have solidified their role as an indispensable component within the RADIUS ecosystem. Network administrators, system integrators, and cybersecurity professionals must fully grasp AVP structures, uses, and best practices to leverage RADIUS effectively within diverse operational contexts. Mastering the nuances of AVPs ensures successful implementation, efficient troubleshooting, and robust security across large-scale, complex network environments, enabling organizations to reliably manage user authentication, authorization, and accounting functions through centralized control mechanisms provided by RADIUS.

Setting Up a RADIUS Server

The process of setting up a RADIUS (Remote Authentication Dial-In User Service) server involves establishing a centralized authentication, authorization, and accounting framework designed to manage network access securely and efficiently. The RADIUS server acts as the central repository for user credentials, policies, and session information, enabling network administrators to control access uniformly across all network entry points, such as wireless access points, VPN gateways, and wired switches. Successfully deploying a RADIUS server requires careful planning, appropriate hardware and software selection, thorough understanding of organizational requirements, and a clear vision of the security objectives intended to be achieved.

Initially, administrators must clearly define the requirements of their network environment, understanding the scope of services needed from the RADIUS server. This involves identifying the types of network devices and users the server must support, the expected volume of authentication requests, and the complexity of authorization policies. Additionally, administrators must consider compatibility with existing infrastructure, integration with directory services or databases like Active Directory or LDAP, and anticipated future expansion. Clarifying these requirements upfront greatly simplifies subsequent setup phases, ensuring that the selected RADIUS solution meets organizational goals and operational realities.

Once requirements are established, administrators must choose suitable hardware and software platforms for hosting the RADIUS server. Hardware specifications will vary depending on expected authentication loads, redundancy needs, and performance requirements. For small or medium-sized networks, modest servers or even virtual machines may suffice, while large enterprise or ISP deployments demand robust, dedicated hardware with sufficient processing power, memory, and high-speed storage. Regarding software, administrators typically select between open-source solutions such as FreeRADIUS or commercial offerings like Microsoft Network Policy Server (NPS) or Cisco ISE. The choice of software is heavily influenced by organizational preferences, budget considerations, required feature sets, ease of integration, and available support.

With hardware and software selected, the next step involves installing and configuring the RADIUS software. Installation typically starts with the underlying operating system setup, often Linux distributions for open-source servers or Windows Server for commercial solutions. Administrators must apply necessary security updates, configure system-level firewall rules, and ensure network connectivity to all relevant NAS devices. Properly configuring networking elements, such as static IP addressing and DNS resolution, is essential for reliable communication between the RADIUS server and client devices across the infrastructure.

Configuring the RADIUS server itself requires establishing the foundational parameters governing authentication interactions. Administrators must define client devices within the RADIUS configuration, specifying details such as NAS IP addresses, shared secrets used to authenticate and encrypt communications, and acceptable authentication methods supported by the RADIUS server. Shared secrets represent a critical security element within RADIUS deployments, providing a layer of confidentiality and integrity protection for packets exchanged between the NAS and the server. Administrators should generate strong, unique shared secrets for each client device, managing these securely to prevent unauthorized access or tampering.

User credential management is another critical aspect of setting up a RADIUS server. Administrators must integrate the server with existing identity repositories or build new databases to store user accounts. Integration with Active Directory or LDAP simplifies credential management in large organizations, allowing administrators to leverage existing infrastructure for centralized user administration. Alternatively, dedicated SQL databases or local user files may be used, particularly in smaller or specialized network environments. Regardless of the chosen method, clearly defining user credentials, passwords, group memberships, and access privileges is crucial to ensuring proper authentication and authorization decisions by the RADIUS server.

Authorization rules must also be meticulously configured within the RADIUS setup. Authorization policies dictate the network resources, access levels, and session constraints granted to users upon successful authentication. Administrators define these rules through explicit attribute-value pairs (AVPs), specifying details such as VLAN assignments, IP address allocations, session timeouts, bandwidth limits, and other access parameters. Properly defined authorization rules ensure consistent enforcement of security policies, enhance network integrity, and streamline administrative management across diverse network access scenarios.

Accounting configuration is another critical element in the setup of a RADIUS server, enabling comprehensive logging and tracking of user activities and session data. Accounting functionality provides administrators with detailed visibility into user sessions, connection durations, data usage, and network resource utilization. Configuring accounting involves defining the frequency of accounting updates, specifying relevant accounting attributes, and ensuring robust storage mechanisms for collected data. Accurate and comprehensive accounting records facilitate compliance auditing, billing purposes, capacity planning, and network security analysis, providing essential insight into network usage patterns and user behavior.

Security considerations underpin every aspect of RADIUS server configuration, necessitating measures such as encrypted communication channels, secure handling of sensitive information, regular security assessments, and timely software updates. Administrators should employ protocols such as IPsec or TLS to encrypt RADIUS communication, safeguarding authentication data from interception. Additionally, restricting physical and logical access to the RADIUS server infrastructure, implementing secure backups, and continuously monitoring server logs for anomalies or potential threats contribute significantly to overall network security.

Finally, testing and validation of the configured RADIUS server represent essential steps in achieving a reliable and secure authentication infrastructure. Administrators should perform comprehensive tests involving simulated user authentication scenarios, authorization policy enforcement, accounting data accuracy, and client-server communication reliability. Rigorous testing uncovers configuration errors, interoperability issues, or potential performance bottlenecks before deployment into a live environment. Post-deployment monitoring ensures ongoing reliability and facilitates prompt identification and resolution of operational issues or emerging security threats, ensuring the RADIUS server continues to effectively manage authentication, authorization, and accounting responsibilities across the network infrastructure.

Configuring Network Access Servers (NAS)

Network Access Servers (NAS) form an essential component within a Remote Authentication Dial-In User Service (RADIUS) deployment, acting as gatekeepers that control access to network resources based on authentication responses from a centralized RADIUS server. Configuring these NAS devices properly is paramount, as they are the critical intermediary between end-users seeking access to a network and the authentication and authorization functions performed by

RADIUS. Effective configuration of NAS devices involves detailed knowledge of their operation, compatibility with RADIUS protocols, and careful attention to security, redundancy, and interoperability considerations, all of which directly impact overall network security and reliability.

The initial step in configuring NAS devices involves establishing connectivity with the central RADIUS server. To enable this, administrators must configure NAS equipment with the necessary details for communication, including specifying the IP addresses or hostnames of primary and secondary RADIUS servers. This ensures that NAS devices correctly route authentication requests and accounting packets to the appropriate destination. In most NAS configurations, administrators must also define the specific RADIUS port numbers for authentication (commonly port 1812 or the legacy port 1645) and accounting services (typically port 1813 or the legacy port 1646). Ensuring correct and consistent use of these standard ports guarantees reliable interoperability and predictable behavior within the broader authentication infrastructure.

A fundamental component of NAS configuration involves the establishment of shared secrets, which are unique security keys used to authenticate and encrypt communications between NAS devices and RADIUS servers. Each NAS device must be individually configured with a secure, unique shared secret that matches precisely the one configured on the corresponding RADIUS server. These secrets provide critical authentication of packets exchanged between NAS and RADIUS servers, preventing unauthorized devices from injecting false authentication data or intercepting sensitive user credentials. Therefore, it is vital to select strong, unpredictable shared secrets, securely distributing and maintaining them within a controlled administrative environment to minimize potential security risks.

Another critical aspect of configuring NAS devices relates to defining supported authentication protocols and methods. NAS configurations typically support various authentication techniques such as Password Authentication Protocol (PAP), Challenge Handshake Authentication Protocol (CHAP), or Extensible Authentication Protocol (EAP). Administrators must explicitly enable and configure these protocols on the NAS, selecting the appropriate authentication mechanisms compatible with user devices and organizational security requirements. For instance, implementing EAP methods such as EAP-TLS or PEAP requires careful configuration to ensure that NAS devices properly handle certificate exchanges and secure tunnels necessary for advanced authentication. Clear understanding and accurate configuration of supported authentication protocols ensure compatibility, security, and seamless user authentication experiences.

Configuring authorization attributes is also an essential responsibility in NAS management. Upon successful authentication of users by the RADIUS server, authorization parameters provided via Attribute-Value Pairs (AVPs) instruct NAS devices on how to handle specific user sessions. Administrators must configure NAS devices to interpret and correctly apply received AVPs, ensuring consistent enforcement of policies related to VLAN assignments, IP address allocations, session timeouts, bandwidth limitations, and permitted services. Properly implemented authorization rules enable network administrators to effectively control and manage network access, enforcing security policies uniformly and dynamically across diverse network entry points and user scenarios.

The configuration of accounting functionality is another critical element in NAS setup. NAS devices must be accurately configured to generate detailed accounting records, documenting user activities, session durations, and resource consumption during network access periods. Accounting records are essential for network monitoring, resource planning, security auditing, and billing purposes, making precise NAS accounting configuration mandatory. Administrators configure parameters such as accounting intervals, triggering conditions for accounting packets, session timeout events, and specific attributes included in accounting messages. Well-configured NAS accounting capabilities ensure administrators have comprehensive visibility into network usage patterns, facilitating efficient management and timely responses to potential security incidents or performance issues.

Security measures within NAS configuration extend beyond authentication settings and shared secrets. NAS devices represent critical points of vulnerability if improperly secured, necessitating stringent security configurations to protect them against unauthorized access, configuration tampering, or malicious attacks. Administrators must configure robust access controls, employing secure administrative access methods such as SSH or secure HTTPS interfaces. Network-level protections, including firewall rules, IP filtering, and port security settings, also play a vital role in securing NAS devices. Regular monitoring of NAS configurations, auditing access logs, and promptly updating software or firmware further enhance the security posture, ensuring that NAS devices reliably support authentication processes without exposing the network to unnecessary risks.

High availability and redundancy configurations are essential for NAS deployments, particularly in large enterprise or ISP environments, where continuous network access is crucial. Administrators should configure NAS devices with failover mechanisms, enabling automatic redirection of authentication requests to secondary RADIUS servers in the event of primary server failures. Load balancing configurations may also be implemented, distributing authentication and accounting requests across multiple RADIUS servers to prevent performance bottlenecks and enhance service reliability. Properly configured redundancy ensures continuous operation, minimizes downtime, and maintains consistent user authentication experiences, critical for maintaining user productivity and overall organizational efficiency.

Continuous testing, monitoring, and maintenance complete the configuration lifecycle of NAS devices within RADIUS infrastructures. Regularly scheduled validation tests ensure proper functioning of authentication, authorization, and accounting configurations, verifying correct interaction between NAS devices and the central RADIUS server. Monitoring real-time NAS logs and accounting data helps identify potential configuration errors, security threats, or performance anomalies, enabling proactive troubleshooting and rapid problem resolution. Ongoing maintenance activities, including periodic configuration reviews, firmware updates, security assessments, and documentation audits, ensure NAS configurations remain optimized, secure, and fully aligned with organizational needs and evolving security standards.

User Authentication Mechanisms

User authentication mechanisms represent fundamental components of network security, ensuring that only authorized individuals or devices can access sensitive resources within organizational networks. Authentication mechanisms encompass a broad range of methodologies designed to verify the identity of users or systems before granting them entry into protected areas of network infrastructure. From basic password-based methods to highly sophisticated, multi-factor and cryptographic solutions, user authentication mechanisms have significantly evolved, driven by escalating threats, growing regulatory compliance requirements, and increased expectations of security among organizations and users alike.

Password-based authentication remains the most familiar and commonly implemented mechanism across various networks and applications. Its popularity stems primarily from simplicity, cost-effectiveness, and ease of deployment, allowing straightforward integration into virtually any network or software environment. Users verify their identities by providing a username and a corresponding password stored in a centralized authentication database. While convenient and widely supported, simple password-based authentication introduces substantial security risks due to vulnerability to attacks such as credential theft, brute-force guessing, phishing, and interception. Password strength requirements, periodic password changes, and hashing passwords during storage mitigate these risks to some extent but fail to entirely eliminate them.

Responding to inherent vulnerabilities associated with simple password authentication, more secure authentication protocols emerged, such as the Challenge Handshake Authentication Protocol (CHAP). CHAP enhances security by eliminating the direct transmission of passwords over networks. Instead, authentication occurs through a challenge-response mechanism. When initiating authentication, the Network Access Server (NAS) issues a random challenge to the user's device. The device responds by combining the challenge with the user's secret password using a cryptographic hash. The server independently calculates the expected response and verifies the user's identity without ever exchanging clear-text credentials. The cryptographic nature of CHAP greatly reduces vulnerability to interception, replay attacks, and credential theft, significantly improving authentication security.

Building upon such improvements, Extensible Authentication Protocol (EAP) provides a versatile framework accommodating numerous advanced authentication mechanisms within network environments. EAP allows flexibility and modularity, supporting authentication methods tailored to specific security and usability requirements. For example, EAP-TLS (Transport Layer Security) employs digital certificates issued by a trusted certificate authority for mutual authentication between client and server. By requiring certificates on both ends, EAP-TLS provides strong identity verification and cryptographic assurance, making it ideal for environments demanding high-security authentication. However, its implementation complexity due to certificate management and Public Key Infrastructure (PKI) requirements can limit adoption in some scenarios.

Alternative EAP methods, such as Protected EAP (PEAP) and EAP-Tunneled TLS (EAP-TTLS), address complexity by encapsulating authentication exchanges within secure encrypted tunnels established between the client and authentication server. With PEAP or EAP-TTLS, only the server requires a certificate, simplifying client-side deployments while maintaining robust authentication security. Users submit credentials securely inside the encrypted tunnel, providing protection against eavesdropping and interception. These tunnel-based mechanisms strike an effective balance between security, simplicity, and practicality, enabling widespread adoption in corporate Wi-Fi, remote-access VPN, and wired network scenarios.

Multi-factor authentication (MFA) mechanisms have gained significant prominence as threats have intensified and traditional single-factor methods have proven insufficient. MFA involves combining multiple authentication factors—something the user knows (password), something the user has (physical token or smartphone), and something the user is (biometric data such as fingerprints or facial recognition). By requiring multiple distinct verification steps, MFA significantly reduces vulnerability to credential compromise, social engineering, or brute-force attacks. Modern MFA implementations increasingly leverage smartphone-based apps, hardware security keys, biometrics, or push notifications, making the additional verification process minimally intrusive while substantially strengthening network security.

Biometric authentication mechanisms have also rapidly evolved, offering secure identification through fingerprint recognition, facial recognition, voice analysis, or iris scanning. These biometrics leverage unique physical or behavioral user characteristics that cannot easily be stolen, replicated, or guessed. Biometrics significantly enhance security and user convenience, reducing reliance on passwords and minimizing associated vulnerabilities. However, biometric data requires rigorous security handling, encryption, and privacy protection, as compromises of biometric databases could have severe, irreversible consequences. Carefully managing biometric deployments, including proper storage practices and regulatory compliance, ensures robust security without sacrificing privacy.

Token-based authentication represents another important mechanism, particularly prevalent in enterprise or high-security scenarios. Hardware or software tokens generate unique, time-sensitive codes or cryptographic keys used to authenticate users. These tokens provide a second authentication factor beyond traditional passwords, greatly mitigating risks associated with credential theft or unauthorized access. The temporary nature of token-generated codes severely limits opportunities for attackers to exploit intercepted or stolen authentication data, significantly improving overall authentication resilience.

Emerging context-aware and adaptive authentication mechanisms represent the next evolution, dynamically adjusting authentication requirements based on real-time analysis of user behavior, device state, geographical location, and other contextual indicators. Adaptive mechanisms recognize unusual login attempts or deviations from typical user patterns, triggering additional verification steps only when elevated risk is detected. This adaptive approach enhances security without unnecessarily burdening legitimate users with excessive verification demands, offering intelligent responsiveness to evolving security threats.

Federated authentication protocols, such as OAuth, OpenID Connect, and Security Assertion Markup Language (SAML), facilitate seamless, secure access across multiple applications or organizations using single sign-on (SSO). These mechanisms allow users to authenticate once with a trusted identity provider, securely granting access to multiple interconnected resources without repeated credential entry. Federated authentication simplifies user experiences, improves productivity, reduces administrative overhead, and enables secure cross-organizational collaboration, all while maintaining robust security controls.

Continuous evolution in authentication mechanisms underscores a persistent drive toward improved network security, enhanced usability, and increased adaptability to emerging threats and user demands. Network administrators and security professionals must thoroughly understand these mechanisms, carefully selecting appropriate authentication solutions based on organizational needs, threat models, regulatory requirements, and user expectations, ensuring secure, efficient, and trustworthy access to critical network resources.

Password Authentication Protocols (PAP)

Password Authentication Protocol (PAP) is one of the earliest and most straightforward authentication methods used in computer networking, originating at a time when simplicity and convenience were prioritized over security. In practice, PAP relies solely on transmitting plaintext usernames and passwords from the user's device or network client to a server for verification. This uncomplicated approach enables rapid and easy deployment in virtually any network environment, contributing to its initial widespread adoption. Despite these practical advantages, PAP's fundamental security flaws have prompted significant shifts toward more secure authentication methodologies, especially as networks have become increasingly susceptible to sophisticated cyber threats.

PAP operates on a basic client-server interaction model. When a user attempts to connect to a network resource, the client initiates the authentication process by sending a request containing the user's username and associated password directly to the authentication server. The server then compares the received credentials against a locally stored or externally maintained user database, such as a text file, LDAP directory, or SQL database. If the username and password combination matches the stored credentials, the server grants network access. If not, the authentication attempt fails, and access is denied. The simplicity of this mechanism is its most appealing feature, making PAP easy to implement across diverse systems, from simple dial-up connections to larger corporate networks.

However, this simplicity also constitutes PAP's greatest vulnerability. Since PAP transmits passwords over network connections in clear text, it offers no inherent protection against interception, eavesdropping, or credential theft. An attacker positioned strategically on the network can easily capture usernames and passwords as they pass through insecure channels. This vulnerability is especially severe in environments such as open wireless networks, public hotspots, or unsecured remote access connections, where intercepting credentials is trivial for cybercriminals or malicious insiders. Consequently, employing PAP without additional protective measures poses a substantial security risk, making it inappropriate as a standalone authentication protocol in modern network contexts.

Recognizing PAP's inherent security weaknesses, network administrators and security professionals have developed practices to mitigate risks when PAP is still required for legacy reasons or specific compatibility needs. One common approach is to secure the transmission channel itself, rather than relying exclusively on PAP for credential protection. For instance, administrators might encapsulate PAP communications within secure protocols such as Transport Layer Security (TLS), Secure Shell (SSH), or Internet Protocol Security (IPsec) tunnels. By encrypting the entire communication channel between client and server, these methods reduce the risk of credential interception, offering enhanced security even when employing a fundamentally insecure authentication protocol like PAP.

Alternatively, some organizations integrate PAP into broader multi-layered security strategies, complementing it with other authentication factors or security mechanisms. For example, even if

PAP remains necessary due to legacy equipment or software constraints, administrators might deploy secondary authentication steps, such as token-based or biometric verification. This multi-factor authentication approach substantially reduces the overall vulnerability associated with PAP, making successful unauthorized access much more difficult. While adding complexity, combining PAP with additional authentication layers or mechanisms allows administrators to balance security requirements with operational realities, maintaining necessary compatibility without sacrificing critical protections.

Despite available mitigations, the limitations and vulnerabilities inherent in PAP have led to the development and widespread adoption of alternative password authentication protocols that significantly improve security. The Challenge Handshake Authentication Protocol (CHAP), for instance, addresses PAP's primary weakness by avoiding the transmission of plaintext passwords entirely. Instead, CHAP uses a cryptographic challenge-response exchange, ensuring passwords never directly traverse the network, significantly enhancing security against interception and replay attacks. Additionally, Extensible Authentication Protocol (EAP) methods, such as EAP-TLS, PEAP, or EAP-TTLS, further advance authentication security through sophisticated encryption techniques, mutual authentication, and secure credential exchanges.

Even with clear alternatives available, understanding PAP remains essential for network administrators, security professionals, and IT teams, particularly due to legacy systems or specific scenarios requiring compatibility. Many older or specialized devices still only support PAP authentication, necessitating a pragmatic approach to security management in these contexts. Administrators working with mixed infrastructure must fully grasp PAP's operation, vulnerabilities, and available protective measures, enabling informed decision-making when integrating legacy technologies into secure networks.

When deploying PAP in any environment, meticulous management practices are critical. Administrators must enforce rigorous password hygiene, mandating strong, complex, and regularly updated passwords to minimize risks associated with credential compromise. Additionally, limiting PAP usage exclusively to strictly controlled and isolated network segments reduces overall exposure, containing potential damage in case of credential theft or interception. Administrators should closely monitor network activity, promptly detecting suspicious login attempts, unauthorized access patterns, or indicators of credential misuse, allowing timely response and mitigation of emerging threats.

Administrators must also consider compliance implications, as modern cybersecurity regulations often mandate stringent authentication standards. Employing PAP without adequate safeguards could violate regulatory requirements, exposing organizations to compliance penalties or legal liabilities. Thoroughly assessing applicable regulations, aligning authentication practices with security standards, and documenting risk mitigation strategies become essential components when incorporating PAP into enterprise security frameworks.

Ultimately, while PAP's simplicity, ease of deployment, and compatibility characteristics continue to offer limited value in specific scenarios, its vulnerabilities necessitate cautious and restricted use. Network administrators should always strive to implement stronger, modern authentication protocols whenever possible, turning to PAP only when no feasible alternative exists. By fully understanding PAP's limitations and carefully managing its deployment through encryption, multi-factor authentication, strict credential management, network segmentation, and proactive monitoring, organizations can minimize associated risks while supporting legacy compatibility needs.

Challenge Handshake Authentication Protocol (CHAP)

The Challenge Handshake Authentication Protocol (CHAP) represents a significant advancement in network authentication methods compared to simpler, less secure protocols such as the Password Authentication Protocol (PAP). Designed to enhance security during user authentication exchanges, CHAP incorporates a cryptographic mechanism that effectively protects passwords and user credentials from interception, replay attacks, and various forms of cyber threats. CHAP achieves its security objectives by employing a challenge-response authentication method, ensuring that sensitive information never travels openly or directly across the network, thereby significantly reducing risks associated with credential compromise.

In a typical CHAP authentication exchange, the authentication process initiates after a client device attempts to establish a network connection with a Network Access Server (NAS). Unlike PAP, which sends clear-text passwords during authentication, CHAP employs a secure handshake process, beginning when the NAS generates and sends a random, unique value—known as the challenge—to the connecting client. Upon receiving the challenge, the client computes a cryptographic hash value using a predetermined cryptographic algorithm (commonly MD5), combining the received challenge with a secret password already known to both the client and the authentication server. The client subsequently returns this calculated hash value, known as the response, back to the NAS for verification.

Upon receiving the client's response, the NAS forwards this response to the authentication server, typically a RADIUS server, where the verification process occurs. The authentication server independently calculates its own hash value based on the challenge previously sent by the NAS and the user's stored secret password retrieved from its authentication database. The server then compares its computed value with the client's response. If both hash values match, the server recognizes that the client possesses the correct password, confirming the user's identity and allowing network access. If the values differ, the authentication fails, resulting in the denial of access to network resources.

A primary strength of CHAP lies in its capability to periodically verify the user's identity during an ongoing network session, rather than relying solely on initial login verification. This ongoing verification is accomplished by periodically repeating the challenge-response exchange at predefined intervals, which helps mitigate the risk of session hijacking, replay attacks, or compromised authentication credentials. Should an attacker intercept previous authentication exchanges, they cannot reuse the intercepted responses, as each challenge-response pair is uniquely generated and valid for a single authentication instance only. Continuous, periodic re-authentication provided by CHAP significantly enhances network security by maintaining rigorous identity validation throughout the duration of each user session.

Another critical security advantage of CHAP arises from the use of cryptographic hashing rather than transmitting plain-text passwords. Hashing ensures the secrecy and integrity of authentication credentials, even if attackers intercept the exchanged packets. Because hash functions are designed to be computationally irreversible, an intercepted CHAP response offers attackers no practical method of determining the original password or secret key. This significantly reduces exposure to credential theft, making CHAP a considerably more secure alternative compared to clear-text protocols such as PAP.

Despite these security advantages, CHAP possesses certain limitations and vulnerabilities that administrators must recognize and address. For instance, CHAP's security strongly depends on the confidentiality of the shared secret password stored at the server and client ends. Therefore, any compromise of stored passwords or weak password management practices significantly undermine CHAP's security posture. Furthermore, CHAP traditionally uses hashing algorithms such as MD5, which, over time, have demonstrated vulnerabilities and susceptibility to collision attacks. Consequently, while still offering improved security over plain-text authentication methods, CHAP implementations benefit from additional security layers, strong password policies, and secure communication channels to ensure adequate protection.

Network administrators deploying CHAP should emphasize strict password management practices, employing strong, unpredictable passwords that reduce vulnerability to brute-force attacks or password guessing. Additionally, administrators must ensure secure handling and storage of authentication credentials, protecting them from unauthorized disclosure or theft. Integrating CHAP within secure encrypted communication channels such as Transport Layer Security (TLS), Secure Shell (SSH), or IPsec further enhances authentication security, providing an additional layer of protection against interception or unauthorized monitoring of CHAP exchanges.

Due to its relative simplicity and compatibility, CHAP remains widely used in various network contexts, particularly in remote access and dial-up authentication scenarios. Legacy networking equipment or older remote access devices frequently maintain compatibility with CHAP, making it essential for network administrators managing mixed or legacy infrastructures. Understanding the operational details, strengths, vulnerabilities, and best practices surrounding CHAP deployment becomes crucial, enabling informed decisions about its suitability and necessary security mitigations.

Modern network environments, however, increasingly favor more secure and robust authentication protocols beyond traditional CHAP, such as advanced Extensible Authentication Protocol (EAP) methods incorporating stronger cryptographic algorithms, mutual authentication, and secure tunnel exchanges. Protocols like EAP-TLS, PEAP, or EAP-TTLS address CHAP's inherent limitations by employing stronger cryptographic protections and eliminating dependency on shared secret passwords. Nonetheless, CHAP's continued relevance, ease of deployment, and improved security compared to basic password authentication methods ensure its ongoing presence and usage in numerous networking scenarios, especially when legacy compatibility constraints exist.

Network administrators and cybersecurity specialists must maintain comprehensive familiarity with CHAP, thoroughly understanding its cryptographic challenge-response mechanism, inherent strengths, and limitations. Properly implemented, managed, and integrated within multi-layered authentication strategies, CHAP continues serving effectively in scenarios requiring secure authentication where more advanced protocols may not be feasible. Careful consideration, robust password management practices, and proactive security measures enable CHAP to fulfill its authentication objectives securely, reliably, and efficiently within contemporary network environments.

Extensible Authentication Protocol (EAP)

Extensible Authentication Protocol (EAP) represents a critical advancement in network authentication mechanisms, delivering unprecedented flexibility, adaptability, and security within contemporary networking environments. Developed initially to overcome limitations inherent in traditional authentication protocols like PAP and CHAP, EAP provides a comprehensive framework capable of supporting numerous authentication methods and cryptographic techniques. By functioning as a versatile protocol container, EAP allows various authentication strategies to coexist seamlessly, adapting dynamically to diverse security requirements across both wired and wireless network infrastructures.

The primary innovation of EAP is its modular architecture, designed explicitly to support an extensive range of authentication methods without needing protocol-level modifications. Rather than dictating a specific authentication mechanism, EAP serves as a standardized transport protocol, facilitating secure exchanges between clients seeking network access and authentication servers verifying user identities. This separation between the protocol framework and individual authentication methods enables administrators to select the most appropriate authentication strategy for their unique environment, facilitating integration of cutting-edge technologies or accommodating legacy systems as needed.

EAP typically operates within a client-server communication model, involving three primary participants: the EAP peer (usually the client device requesting network access), the authenticator (often a Network Access Server or NAS device managing access), and the authentication server (such as a RADIUS server). Authentication exchanges begin when the EAP peer initiates a network connection request, prompting the authenticator to request identity information. After the peer provides this identity, the authenticator forwards it to the authentication server, initiating a structured dialogue to negotiate and carry out the chosen authentication method. Throughout the authentication exchange, EAP transparently transports authentication messages between the client and authentication server, supporting various cryptographic methods, challenges, responses, and encrypted communications.

Among the numerous authentication methods available under the EAP umbrella, EAP-Transport Layer Security (EAP-TLS) represents one of the most secure and widely deployed methods, offering robust mutual authentication and cryptographic assurance. EAP-TLS requires both client and authentication server to possess valid digital certificates issued by a trusted certificate authority (CA). During the authentication process, EAP-TLS exchanges certificates securely, verifying each party's identity through cryptographic means. This certificate-based approach significantly enhances security, as authentication relies on robust cryptographic keys rather than potentially compromised or guessable passwords. However, deploying EAP-TLS introduces complexity related to certificate management, distribution, and revocation, often necessitating a fully operational Public Key Infrastructure (PKI).

Recognizing the complexity associated with EAP-TLS certificate management, alternative EAP methods like Protected EAP (PEAP) and EAP-Tunneled TLS (EAP-TTLS) emerged to simplify deployment while maintaining high-security standards. PEAP and EAP-TTLS authenticate the authentication server using certificates, establishing secure encrypted tunnels for subsequent exchanges between client and server. Once this secure channel is established, the client securely transmits traditional authentication credentials, such as passwords, within the encrypted tunnel. This approach considerably reduces exposure risks associated with transmitting passwords openly over networks, eliminating the complexity of managing individual client certificates required by EAP-TLS.

The widespread adoption of Wi-Fi and wireless networks significantly increased reliance on EAP as a primary authentication framework. Integration of EAP within IEEE 802.1X frameworks has become standard practice, providing robust access control for wireless networks. EAP authentication integrated with 802.1X ensures rigorous validation of users attempting to connect, preventing unauthorized devices from accessing network resources. In wireless environments, methods such as PEAP, EAP-TTLS, or EAP-TLS have become the standard due to their secure tunnel capabilities, cryptographic assurances, and resistance to common wireless attacks such as rogue access points or man-in-the-middle attempts.

EAP's extensible design supports innovative authentication strategies, including token-based authentication, multi-factor authentication (MFA), and biometric methods, further enhancing overall network security. Organizations increasingly incorporate MFA strategies within EAP, leveraging smartphones, hardware tokens, and biometric identification to supplement traditional passwords. By combining multiple distinct authentication factors, EAP-based MFA implementations substantially strengthen security, dramatically reducing vulnerability to credential theft, phishing attacks, or unauthorized access.

Beyond traditional enterprise and wireless environments, EAP is increasingly critical within advanced networking paradigms such as virtual private networks (VPNs), cloud-based infrastructure, and mobile networks. EAP's adaptable framework allows seamless integration of authentication across diverse network types, enabling consistent security policies regardless of connection context. For instance, VPN deployments often rely on EAP-based authentication to verify remote users securely, maintaining stringent identity validation across geographically dispersed infrastructures. Mobile network providers similarly utilize EAP for authenticating subscribers, providing secure, scalable, and manageable authentication within cellular data networks.

Despite these advantages, successful EAP deployment demands careful consideration of compatibility, performance, and security trade-offs inherent in chosen authentication methods. Administrators must thoroughly evaluate available EAP methods, carefully selecting options aligned with organizational security requirements, available infrastructure, user experience considerations, and overall operational goals. Rigorous testing and validation procedures are essential to ensure seamless client-server interoperability, reliable performance, and robust security within EAP-enabled networks.

Implementing EAP also mandates meticulous management practices surrounding cryptographic certificates, key generation, distribution, revocation, and renewal processes. Effective certificate lifecycle management ensures continued trustworthiness of authentication credentials, preventing potential disruptions, vulnerabilities, or unauthorized access due to expired or compromised certificates. Administrators must integrate comprehensive monitoring, logging, and incident response capabilities within EAP implementations, enabling prompt detection, diagnosis, and mitigation of potential authentication anomalies, attacks, or configuration errors.

As network security threats evolve, EAP continues adapting dynamically, incorporating stronger cryptographic techniques, advanced authentication methods, and improved security protections. Network administrators and cybersecurity professionals must remain informed about ongoing EAP developments, continuously evaluating and optimizing EAP implementations within their environments. A comprehensive understanding of EAP's extensible architecture, authentication methodologies, security benefits, and operational complexities ensures secure, scalable, and future-proof authentication strategies across diverse networking infrastructures.

RADIUS and 802.1X Integration

The integration of Remote Authentication Dial-In User Service (RADIUS) with the IEEE 802.1X standard represents a pivotal development in securing modern wired and wireless networks. This integration provides robust and scalable mechanisms for authenticating and authorizing users attempting network access, significantly enhancing network security by enforcing strict identity validation at the network edge. RADIUS and 802.1X work together seamlessly to ensure that only authenticated and authorized devices gain entry to network resources, reducing risks associated with unauthorized access, rogue devices, and potential intrusions. By combining these two widely adopted technologies, administrators achieve centralized control, streamlined management, and consistent security policies across both wired and wireless infrastructure.

IEEE 802.1X serves as the primary standard for network access control at the port level, ensuring users and devices must authenticate successfully before gaining full network connectivity. At its core, 802.1X employs a client-server authentication model consisting of three key entities: the supplicant, authenticator, and authentication server. The supplicant refers to the user's client device requesting network access, the authenticator typically represents a network access point such as a switch or wireless access point controlling connectivity, and the authentication server is often implemented using a RADIUS server responsible for validating credentials provided by the supplicant. Together, these components coordinate to verify identities securely before granting or denying network access.

When a user or device attempts to access an 802.1X-enabled network port or wireless network, the authenticator immediately initiates the authentication process. Initially, the authenticator maintains the network port in an unauthorized state, restricting traffic strictly to authentication-related exchanges until identity validation completes successfully. Upon detecting an access attempt, the authenticator forwards an authentication request from the supplicant to the centralized RADIUS server. Using RADIUS as the authentication backend, the authenticator communicates securely with the RADIUS server, passing credential information and authentication exchanges via RADIUS packets, relying on encrypted channels to maintain confidentiality and integrity.

Once the RADIUS server receives an authentication request, it evaluates the provided credentials against a centralized user database, which may include Active Directory, LDAP directories, or SQL databases containing user accounts, passwords, and permissions. This centralized credential management significantly simplifies administrative responsibilities by enabling uniform enforcement of security policies and reducing configuration complexity across diverse network access devices. The RADIUS server analyzes authentication credentials, performs verification using specified authentication methods such as EAP-TLS, PEAP, or EAP-TTLS, and returns a response indicating success or failure back to the authenticator device. The authenticator then allows or denies network connectivity based upon the outcome communicated by the RADIUS server.

In addition to authentication, the integration of RADIUS with 802.1X facilitates powerful authorization capabilities, enabling detailed control over user access parameters through Attribute-Value Pairs (AVPs). Upon successful authentication, the RADIUS server returns AVPs specifying specific access conditions, privileges, and session limitations. Examples include dynamic VLAN assignments, IP address allocations, quality-of-service parameters, bandwidth restrictions, and session duration constraints. Network access devices implementing

802.1X interpret and enforce these authorization attributes precisely, ensuring compliance with organizational policies and maintaining rigorous security standards across all network entry points.

Accounting capabilities represent another critical advantage achieved through integrating RADIUS with 802.1X. Network administrators leverage RADIUS accounting functionality to collect comprehensive session data, user activity logs, and detailed network usage information. Authenticator devices transmit accounting packets to the RADIUS server, documenting session start and stop times, total data transferred, connection durations, and additional session details. Centralized accounting data provides administrators with valuable insights for auditing, compliance monitoring, resource planning, and security investigations, significantly enhancing overall network visibility and management efficiency.

Wireless network environments have particularly benefited from integrating RADIUS and 802.1X, addressing numerous security vulnerabilities previously associated with open or weakly secured Wi-Fi deployments. The adoption of WPA2-Enterprise (Wi-Fi Protected Access 2 with 802.1X authentication) has become standard practice within enterprise wireless deployments, enforcing rigorous identity verification through secure EAP methods backed by RADIUS servers. By implementing WPA2-Enterprise and 802.1X authentication with centralized RADIUS management, organizations significantly mitigate risks associated with unauthorized wireless access, rogue access points, credential interception, and network intrusion attempts.

Similarly, wired network environments leverage 802.1X and RADIUS integration to prevent unauthorized access through physical Ethernet ports, enhancing physical and logical security. Organizations deploying 802.1X on switches ensure that unauthorized devices cannot easily connect to internal networks, effectively preventing potential insider threats or unauthorized hardware. In such deployments, switch ports remain blocked or quarantined until successful authentication occurs via RADIUS, ensuring consistent and enforceable security policies at every physical network connection point.

Successful integration of RADIUS with 802.1X demands careful configuration, comprehensive testing, and ongoing maintenance.

Administrators must configure authenticator devices correctly, specifying RADIUS server details, shared secrets, supported EAP authentication methods, and authorization parameters. Correctly deploying digital certificates and secure communication channels between authenticators and RADIUS servers is paramount, as misconfigurations may compromise overall security. Rigorous testing and validation ensure seamless interoperability, reliable authentication, and accurate authorization enforcement across network infrastructure, minimizing potential disruptions or vulnerabilities.

Administrators must also manage redundancy and fault-tolerance configurations effectively, implementing backup RADIUS servers, load balancing mechanisms, and failover procedures to ensure continuous network availability and security even during server outages or failures. Proactive monitoring and logging practices further enhance integration security, promptly identifying and addressing suspicious activities, authentication failures, configuration anomalies, or potential threats, enabling rapid and effective incident responses.

The powerful combination of RADIUS and 802.1X continues evolving, adapting dynamically to emerging networking paradigms such as cloud infrastructure, IoT deployments, and evolving wireless technologies. Continuous improvements in cryptographic techniques, authentication methods, security protocols, and interoperability standards ensure ongoing relevance and efficacy of RADIUS and 802.1X integration within rapidly changing technological landscapes. Network administrators and cybersecurity specialists must maintain comprehensive familiarity with this integration, continuously optimizing deployments, security configurations, and operational practices to achieve secure, efficient, and scalable authentication infrastructures capable of addressing contemporary network security challenges.

Wired Network Authentication with RADIUS

Wired network authentication using Remote Authentication Dial-In User Service (RADIUS) has become an essential practice for securing network infrastructure, particularly in enterprise environments where security and access control are paramount. Implementing RADIUS authentication in wired networks provides administrators with centralized management of user identities and policies, significantly enhancing security by ensuring that only authenticated and authorized devices gain access to network resources. The integration of RADIUS in wired network scenarios enforces rigorous validation of identities at each network access point, thereby reducing vulnerabilities related to unauthorized or unmanaged connections.

Traditional wired networks often lacked adequate access control mechanisms, allowing virtually any device physically connected to a network port to access internal resources. This scenario posed substantial risks, including unauthorized access, insider threats, and potential data breaches. To address these vulnerabilities, organizations began deploying RADIUS-based authentication combined with IEEE 802.1X network access control. This integration provides a robust mechanism to authenticate devices before granting network connectivity. Specifically, it ensures that the authentication process occurs at the network port level, blocking unauthorized devices from connecting until authentication is successfully completed.

In wired networks secured by RADIUS, the authentication process begins as soon as a user or device physically connects to an Ethernet port on a network switch configured with 802.1X capabilities. At this point, the port remains in an unauthorized state, meaning no network traffic except authentication data can pass through. The network switch acts as an authenticator, initiating an authentication request and immediately communicating with a centralized RADIUS server. The authenticator forwards credential information provided by the connecting device, typically encapsulated using Extensible Authentication Protocol (EAP), to the RADIUS server for validation.

Upon receiving authentication data, the RADIUS server verifies the identity of the connecting device or user by referencing a centralized credential store, such as Active Directory, LDAP directory services, or a SQL database containing user accounts and permissions. The RADIUS server utilizes configured authentication methods, such as EAP-TLS, PEAP, or EAP-TTLS, to securely validate the provided credentials. After completing authentication verification, the RADIUS server sends an authentication response back to the authenticator, either granting or denying access based on credential validity and defined policies.

The ability to dynamically assign network parameters represents one of the significant advantages of wired network authentication with RADIUS. After successful authentication, the RADIUS server communicates specific authorization attributes back to the authenticator device using Attribute-Value Pairs (AVPs). These attributes detail precise instructions regarding network access privileges, VLAN assignments, IP address allocations, session durations, bandwidth limitations, and other critical access conditions. Network switches interpret these authorization attributes, ensuring that authenticated devices receive appropriate network resources aligned with organizational policies and security standards. Dynamic VLAN assignment, for example, automatically places users or devices into VLANs based on their identities or roles, significantly streamlining administrative efforts and enhancing security segmentation.

Accounting functionality integrated within RADIUS authentication also provides comprehensive session monitoring and logging capabilities in wired networks. Each session authenticated through RADIUS generates detailed accounting records documenting the duration of connections, session initiation and termination timestamps, data transfer volumes, and relevant network activity details. Centralized accounting records maintained by RADIUS servers enable administrators to analyze user activities, detect potential security issues, ensure compliance with organizational policies, and optimize network resource usage.

Security considerations form an integral aspect of deploying wired network authentication using RADIUS. Communication between network switches (authenticators) and RADIUS servers must be adequately secured to prevent credential interception or unauthorized packet manipulation. Administrators typically use secure communication channels, such as IPsec tunnels or encrypted TLS connections, to safeguard RADIUS exchanges, ensuring data confidentiality and integrity. Furthermore, robust shared secrets configured between authenticators and RADIUS servers provide cryptographic validation of transmitted packets, protecting against spoofing and replay attacks.

High availability and redundancy mechanisms are essential for maintaining reliable wired network authentication infrastructures. Administrators commonly deploy redundant RADIUS servers, configured in failover pairs or load-balanced clusters, ensuring continuous availability of authentication services even during primary server outages or maintenance periods. Network switches supporting RADIUS typically offer configurable backup server options, automatically redirecting authentication requests to secondary servers when the primary is unavailable. Such redundancy ensures uninterrupted access control, maintaining consistent security enforcement across wired network environments.

Careful management practices are crucial when deploying RADIUS-based wired network authentication, particularly regarding credential management, authentication method selection, and operational maintenance. Administrators must implement robust password policies, certificate management procedures, and multi-factor authentication strategies to strengthen overall security posture. Rigorous testing and validation of RADIUS and 802.1X configurations ensure reliable and secure interoperability between network switches, authentication servers, and user devices, minimizing operational disruptions and security vulnerabilities.

Additionally, proactive monitoring, logging, and incident response capabilities further enhance the effectiveness of wired network authentication with RADIUS. Detailed logging of authentication attempts, authorization decisions, and session activities provides critical insights for troubleshooting, security investigations, and compliance auditing. Real-time monitoring enables administrators to promptly identify and respond to unauthorized access attempts, authentication failures, configuration anomalies, or suspicious activities, significantly improving organizational responsiveness to potential security incidents.

Modern enterprises continue adopting wired network authentication with RADIUS as part of broader network security strategies. Advances in technology, such as network access control (NAC) solutions integrated with RADIUS authentication, further enhance wired network security by enabling advanced policy enforcement, endpoint compliance checks, and automated remediation capabilities. NAC solutions leveraging RADIUS authentication can verify endpoint security posture before granting network access, ensuring connected devices meet established security standards, such as updated antivirus software or compliance with specific security configurations.

The deployment of wired network authentication using RADIUS consistently demonstrates measurable improvements in organizational security, administrative efficiency, and network visibility. As threats evolve and network infrastructure complexity increases, organizations will rely increasingly on robust authentication solutions combining RADIUS and IEEE 802.1X standards. Continuous improvements in cryptographic techniques, authentication methods, and interoperability standards ensure ongoing relevance and efficacy of wired network authentication with RADIUS, helping enterprises effectively address contemporary cybersecurity challenges and securely manage network access.

Wireless Network Authentication

Wireless network authentication has evolved considerably over recent years, becoming a crucial aspect of modern network security management. Ensuring that wireless access is secure, reliable, and properly controlled represents a primary concern for organizations and network administrators, particularly given the widespread adoption of mobile devices, remote working scenarios, and the increasing need for mobility within corporate environments. Unlike wired networks, wireless networks inherently transmit data over radio frequencies, making them especially susceptible to interception, unauthorized access, and other cybersecurity threats. As a result, implementing robust authentication methods specifically designed for wireless networks has become essential in mitigating risks and maintaining network integrity.

Initially, wireless networks depended largely on simple authentication methods, primarily relying on shared passwords and static encryption keys. The earliest standard for wireless security, known as Wired Equivalent Privacy (WEP), attempted to provide basic authentication and confidentiality through static encryption. However, due to significant cryptographic weaknesses, WEP proved vulnerable to easy exploitation, prompting organizations and standards bodies to seek more secure alternatives. This early failure highlighted the necessity for robust authentication methods specifically tailored to address the unique challenges of wireless networks, such as ease of interception and unauthorized device connections.

Responding to these challenges, the introduction of Wi-Fi Protected Access (WPA) marked a major improvement in wireless authentication and security. WPA improved upon WEP by implementing more secure encryption methods, particularly Temporal Key Integrity Protocol (TKIP), which dynamically generated encryption keys and provided better protection against common wireless attacks. However, the most significant enhancement introduced by WPA—and further refined in WPA2—was the adoption of WPA-Enterprise, which leveraged IEEE 802.1X authentication integrated with Remote Authentication Dial-In User Service (RADIUS) servers. WPA-Enterprise significantly strengthened authentication by requiring individual user authentication rather than shared network passwords, thus dramatically reducing risks associated with unauthorized access, credential compromise, or brute-force attacks.

In WPA-Enterprise environments, wireless network authentication follows a well-defined process involving multiple key entities: wireless clients (supplicants), wireless access points (authenticators), and centralized RADIUS authentication servers. When a wireless client attempts to connect, the access point initially restricts all network traffic to authentication exchanges. The client then submits identity information to the access point, which immediately forwards the request securely to the RADIUS server. The authentication server validates the client's credentials using predefined authentication methods, such as Extensible Authentication Protocol (EAP) variants like EAP-TLS, PEAP, or EAP-TTLS. Upon successful validation, the RADIUS server sends an access-granted response containing authorization attributes back to the wireless access point, which subsequently enables full network access for the authenticated client.

EAP methods play a central role in modern wireless authentication, providing secure credential exchange mechanisms that protect sensitive authentication data from interception or manipulation. Among these methods, EAP-TLS remains particularly effective, employing mutual certificate-based authentication between clients and authentication servers. Both entities must possess valid digital certificates, enabling strong identity verification through cryptographic mechanisms rather than traditional passwords. This method ensures robust wireless security but requires careful certificate management and Public Key Infrastructure (PKI) deployment, making its implementation complex but highly secure.

To simplify wireless network authentication deployments without sacrificing security, many organizations adopt methods such as Protected EAP (PEAP) or EAP-Tunneled TLS (EAP-TTLS). These authentication strategies simplify client-side requirements by only mandating server-side certificates, establishing secure, encrypted tunnels for transmitting traditional user credentials. This encrypted tunnel prevents attackers from intercepting authentication data, significantly enhancing wireless security compared to traditional shared-key approaches or basic password methods. As a result, PEAP and EAP-TTLS have become widespread standards in enterprise wireless network authentication scenarios, balancing ease of deployment with strong cryptographic assurances.

Integrating RADIUS authentication into wireless networks provides significant administrative advantages by centralizing authentication management, policy enforcement, and session monitoring. RADIUS servers maintain centralized credential stores, often integrating seamlessly with existing identity management infrastructure, including Active Directory or LDAP directories. This centralization simplifies user administration, reduces configuration complexity across multiple access points, and ensures uniform enforcement of security policies. Furthermore, centralized RADIUS accounting functionality enables comprehensive logging of wireless session activities, providing administrators detailed insights into network usage, facilitating auditing, compliance monitoring, and proactive security analysis.

Security considerations extend beyond authentication methods and encompass comprehensive strategies to secure wireless communication channels and devices themselves. Modern wireless deployments typically leverage WPA2 or WPA3 standards combined with strong cryptographic algorithms, including AES encryption, to protect data transmitted across wireless networks. Administrators further enhance wireless security through rigorous access control policies, intrusion detection systems (IDS), wireless intrusion prevention systems (WIPS), and proactive vulnerability management practices, mitigating risks associated with rogue access points, man-in-the-middle attacks, and wireless denial-of-service incidents.

Wireless network authentication has also benefited significantly from advances in multi-factor authentication (MFA) and adaptive security technologies. Increasingly, organizations deploy MFA within wireless networks, combining traditional authentication credentials with additional verification methods such as biometric authentication, hardware tokens, or smartphone-based applications. MFA significantly reduces vulnerability to credential compromise or unauthorized access attempts, further strengthening wireless security. Adaptive authentication strategies dynamically assess contextual information such as user location, device type, and connection history, allowing networks to adjust authentication requirements based on real-time risk assessments, effectively balancing security with user convenience.

Continuous improvements in wireless network authentication reflect evolving cybersecurity threats, technological advances, and changing user expectations. Administrators must stay informed about emerging authentication protocols, cryptographic standards, and security best practices, regularly updating wireless deployments accordingly. Comprehensive training and awareness programs educate users about secure wireless practices, credential management, and potential risks associated with wireless connectivity, ensuring an informed, security-conscious user population.

Ultimately, wireless network authentication remains a dynamic and essential aspect of modern network security strategy. Organizations investing in robust wireless authentication methods significantly reduce their exposure to security threats, improve overall network integrity, and enhance administrative efficiency. As wireless technologies evolve, ongoing developments in authentication standards, cryptographic protections, and security integration promise continued improvements in secure, reliable, and scalable wireless networking solutions suitable for addressing future cybersecurity challenges.

RADIUS in VPN Networks

The integration of Remote Authentication Dial-In User Service (RADIUS) within Virtual Private Networks (VPN) has become increasingly important as organizations embrace remote workforces, mobile connectivity, and distributed business operations. VPN technology establishes secure, encrypted connections over public networks, such as the internet, allowing remote users to access sensitive internal resources securely from external locations. By incorporating RADIUS into VPN authentication processes, organizations achieve centralized identity management, streamlined administrative control, and significantly improved network security. RADIUS serves as a core component in securing VPN connections, ensuring that only authenticated and authorized users gain access to corporate networks and confidential data.

In typical VPN deployments without centralized authentication, managing user credentials and authorization policies quickly becomes complex, particularly when scaling to support numerous remote employees or distributed office locations. Each VPN gateway traditionally maintains its own set of local authentication credentials, causing administrative overhead, increased complexity, and potential security vulnerabilities associated with inconsistent credential management. Incorporating RADIUS into VPN infrastructures solves this complexity by centralizing authentication, authorization, and accounting services, simplifying credential management, and ensuring consistent policy enforcement across all VPN entry points.

When a remote user initiates a VPN connection request, the VPN gateway acts as a Network Access Server (NAS), serving as the authentication intermediary between the remote client and the centralized RADIUS server. The VPN gateway forwards the user's authentication request, including login credentials such as username, password, or digital certificates, directly to the RADIUS server. The RADIUS server, upon receiving the authentication request, evaluates the provided credentials against a centralized user database, which often integrates seamlessly with existing identity management solutions such as Active Directory, LDAP directories, or SQL databases. By leveraging these centralized credential repositories, administrators efficiently manage user identities, passwords, permissions, and authentication policies, reducing complexity and improving security control.

After verifying user credentials, the RADIUS server returns an authentication response to the VPN gateway, indicating success or failure based on predefined authentication policies. Upon successful authentication, RADIUS communicates precise authorization parameters back to the VPN gateway using Attribute-Value Pairs (AVPs). These AVPs specify detailed access rules, session attributes, and network resources granted to the authenticated user, including dynamically assigned IP addresses, permitted network segments, session timeouts, and bandwidth restrictions. The VPN gateway interprets and applies these authorization attributes accurately, ensuring authenticated users receive appropriate privileges and resources aligned with organizational security policies.

Incorporating RADIUS into VPN networks also introduces essential accounting functionality, enabling detailed monitoring, logging, and analysis of remote connection activities. VPN gateways transmit accounting packets to the centralized RADIUS server, documenting comprehensive session details such as session duration, data transferred, login and logout timestamps, and other relevant user activities. Centralized accounting records facilitate critical functions like auditing, compliance verification, resource allocation planning, and security investigations. Accurate and detailed accounting ensures organizations maintain visibility into remote user activities, network usage patterns, and potential security anomalies, enabling proactive responses to emerging security threats or policy violations.

Security considerations play a critical role when integrating RADIUS with VPN infrastructures, given the sensitive nature of authentication credentials, authorization parameters, and transmitted accounting data. To safeguard communications between VPN gateways and RADIUS servers, administrators commonly implement secure communication channels such as encrypted Transport Layer Security (TLS) connections or IPsec tunnels. Robust cryptographic protection ensures confidentiality and integrity of authentication data transmitted over public or private networks, reducing risks associated with interception, unauthorized access, or packet manipulation.

Additionally, deploying strong authentication methods within VPN-RADIUS integrations significantly enhances overall network security. Modern VPN solutions typically support advanced authentication protocols such as Extensible Authentication Protocol (EAP), providing secure credential exchange mechanisms that prevent sensitive information from exposure. Popular EAP variants, including EAP-TLS, PEAP, and EAP-TTLS, offer robust cryptographic assurances, mutual certificate-based authentication, and secure credential transmission channels. Organizations frequently combine these strong authentication protocols with Multi-Factor Authentication (MFA) strategies, integrating hardware tokens, smartphone-based apps, or biometric verification methods. Implementing MFA alongside RADIUS-based authentication significantly reduces risks related to compromised credentials, unauthorized access attempts, or identity spoofing.

Redundancy and high-availability configurations are critical elements of effective RADIUS deployment within VPN networks, ensuring uninterrupted authentication services during server outages or network disruptions. Administrators often deploy redundant RADIUS servers, configured in active-passive or load-balanced configurations, to maintain continuous VPN authentication availability. VPN gateways typically support multiple RADIUS server definitions, automatically redirecting authentication requests to secondary or backup servers if primary RADIUS servers become unreachable. Such redundancy strategies ensure continuous VPN access control, maintaining consistent security enforcement and uninterrupted remote connectivity.

Proactive monitoring, logging, and incident response strategies further strengthen VPN network security integrated with RADIUS authentication. Comprehensive logging of VPN authentication attempts, authorization decisions, and user sessions provides essential insights into remote access activities, enabling administrators to detect suspicious login attempts, repeated authentication failures, unauthorized access patterns, or anomalous behaviors promptly. Real-time monitoring tools, integrated with RADIUS accounting data, facilitate early detection of security incidents, configuration errors, or resource bottlenecks, enabling administrators to respond rapidly and decisively to emerging issues.

VPN networks increasingly integrate with advanced network access control (NAC) solutions utilizing RADIUS authentication to enforce endpoint compliance checks, ensuring remote devices connecting via VPN meet established security policies. NAC solutions verify endpoint security posture, ensuring devices have updated antivirus software, required operating system patches, or mandated security configurations before granting VPN access. Integrating NAC with RADIUS authentication further enhances security by preventing vulnerable or compromised devices from accessing sensitive corporate networks.

Continuous advancements in VPN and RADIUS integration highlight ongoing improvements in cryptographic standards, authentication methodologies, interoperability protocols, and security best practices. Network administrators must regularly evaluate and optimize their VPN-RADIUS deployments, updating authentication methods, securing communication channels, enhancing redundancy configurations, and maintaining rigorous monitoring practices. Organizations leveraging RADIUS-based VPN authentication benefit significantly from centralized identity management, streamlined administration, robust security enforcement, and comprehensive visibility into remote user activities, effectively addressing contemporary cybersecurity challenges associated with remote and mobile workforces.

Managing User Access Levels

Managing user access levels is a crucial element in ensuring secure and efficient network operation within any organization. Effective access level management ensures that users are granted precisely the privileges required to perform their specific roles, preventing unauthorized access to sensitive resources and minimizing the potential damage arising from insider threats or compromised credentials. Centralized control over user permissions not only streamlines administrative workflows but also significantly enhances overall security by enforcing consistent, well-defined policies across various network entry points. As networks become increasingly complex, distributed, and interconnected, properly managing user access levels grows even more essential in maintaining robust security and operational efficiency.

Centralized authentication solutions such as Remote Authentication Dial-In User Service (RADIUS) provide administrators with powerful mechanisms for controlling and enforcing user access levels across organizational networks. By leveraging RADIUS, administrators can centrally define, modify, and enforce access policies, privileges, and restrictions, effectively aligning user access with organizational roles, responsibilities, and security requirements. When users authenticate through RADIUS, the system verifies credentials and immediately communicates precise authorization parameters to network access devices using Attribute-Value Pairs (AVPs). These AVPs specify user-specific access conditions, including permitted resources, session limitations, bandwidth restrictions, and other relevant authorization details, ensuring each user receives access tailored specifically to their role within the organization.

Role-based access control (RBAC) represents one widely adopted approach for effectively managing user access levels within RADIUS-enabled networks. RBAC simplifies permission management by associating users with predefined roles reflecting their organizational responsibilities or job functions. Administrators first define roles based on organizational hierarchy, functional requirements, or security considerations, assigning specific access privileges and restrictions to each defined role. Individual users are subsequently assigned to appropriate roles rather than directly granting or modifying permissions at the user level. RBAC significantly reduces administrative overhead by streamlining permission assignment processes, enabling administrators to rapidly adjust user privileges, enforce consistent security policies, and simplify overall management of network access.

In addition to RBAC, many organizations implement group-based access control to efficiently manage user access levels. Similar to RBAC, group-based control allows administrators to assign permissions collectively to groups of users sharing common characteristics, responsibilities, or security profiles. Groups might correspond to organizational departments, teams, project assignments, or specialized roles. Administrators assign permissions once at the group level, automatically extending those privileges to all group members. By structuring access permissions around groups rather than individuals, administrators achieve greater efficiency, consistency, and accuracy in managing permissions, ensuring rapid responsiveness to organizational changes or evolving security requirements.

Managing user access levels also involves dynamically assigning network parameters to authenticated users. When users authenticate through a centralized authentication server such as RADIUS, authorization attributes communicated to network access devices can specify dynamic configurations, including VLAN assignments, IP addresses, or session parameters. Dynamic VLAN assignments allow administrators to place users into appropriate network segments based explicitly on roles or group memberships, enhancing network segmentation and security controls. Similarly, dynamic IP address allocation enables efficient resource management, ensuring users receive necessary network resources aligned precisely with their access privileges and session requirements.

Detailed monitoring and logging capabilities represent essential aspects of effective user access management, providing administrators with comprehensive visibility into user activities, permission usage, and potential security incidents. Centralized authentication and authorization systems typically maintain detailed logs documenting authentication attempts, authorization decisions, and user session details. This logging provides administrators with valuable insights into access patterns, compliance verification, resource usage, and potential security anomalies. Real-time monitoring and proactive analysis of log data enable administrators to rapidly identify and address unauthorized access attempts, permission abuses, or suspicious behaviors, significantly enhancing organizational security posture and enabling timely, effective incident responses.

Additionally, adaptive and contextual access control techniques further enhance the management of user access levels by dynamically adjusting privileges based on real-time context, risk assessment, or user behavior analytics. Context-aware access control considers multiple contextual factors, including user location, device type, network state, time of access, or historical behavior patterns, dynamically modifying access privileges or initiating additional verification steps when detecting elevated risk scenarios. Adaptive authentication methods automatically enforce additional authentication requirements, such as multi-factor authentication (MFA), when accessing sensitive resources, detecting unusual user behavior, or recognizing potentially compromised credentials. Implementing adaptive and context-aware access control methods significantly enhances security responsiveness, balancing rigorous security requirements with user convenience and productivity.

Comprehensive lifecycle management processes also remain crucial in managing user access levels effectively, ensuring permissions accurately reflect current organizational roles, responsibilities, or employment statuses. Lifecycle management practices encompass user provisioning, ongoing permission review processes, regular access recertification, and timely de-provisioning upon role changes or employee departures. Regular access recertification processes periodically validate assigned privileges, ensuring continued alignment between organizational responsibilities and granted permissions. Timely provisioning and de-provisioning reduce exposure to unauthorized access, credential misuse, or potential security breaches, maintaining security integrity as organizational roles evolve.

High-level integration between authentication systems, identity management solutions, and organizational directories further streamlines user access management, providing administrators with centralized control, streamlined workflows, and consistent security policy enforcement. Integrating authentication systems such as

RADIUS with centralized identity repositories like Active Directory, LDAP directories, or HR management systems simplifies credential synchronization, user provisioning, role assignment, and permission updates. Centralized integration reduces administrative complexity, ensures rapid responsiveness to organizational changes, and provides comprehensive visibility into user access and permission management across the enterprise.

Continuous training and awareness programs further support effective user access management by educating administrators, managers, and end-users about secure credential management, permission requirements, access policies, and potential security risks associated with improper permissions or credential misuse. Educating users about security responsibilities, appropriate resource usage, and secure authentication practices ensures informed compliance with organizational access policies, reducing accidental breaches or unauthorized access resulting from negligence, misunderstanding, or misuse.

Overall, effectively managing user access levels involves comprehensive strategies encompassing centralized authentication control, role-based or group-based access management, dynamic network parameter assignments, rigorous monitoring practices, adaptive and context-aware access control techniques, lifecycle management processes, identity system integration, and user education initiatives. Implementing robust user access management practices significantly enhances organizational security posture, reduces administrative complexity, maintains regulatory compliance, and ensures secure, efficient operation within complex and dynamic network environments.

Implementing Authorization Policies

Implementing authorization policies effectively is a fundamental aspect of maintaining robust security controls and operational efficiency in network management. Authorization policies define precisely what resources, privileges, and capabilities are accessible to authenticated users or devices, ensuring access aligns strictly with organizational roles, security requirements, and compliance standards. While authentication validates user identity, authorization explicitly governs permitted activities post-authentication, making it vital to overall security and resource management. Organizations deploying centralized authorization methods, particularly utilizing protocols such as Remote Authentication Dial-In User Service (RADIUS), achieve consistent, dynamic, and secure enforcement of these policies across diverse networking environments.

Authorization policies typically encompass multiple elements, including network resources accessible by users, session parameters, application-level permissions, and access restrictions tailored specifically to organizational requirements. Effective authorization policies reflect the organization's internal structure, job responsibilities, regulatory compliance obligations, and security posture. Clearly defined policies ensure users receive appropriate access necessary for productivity while simultaneously preventing unauthorized access or privilege escalation that could lead to security breaches or compliance violations.

Centralized authentication servers, such as RADIUS, enable streamlined implementation and enforcement of authorization policies, simplifying administrative tasks while improving security consistency. After successful authentication, the RADIUS server communicates specific authorization instructions directly to network access devices through Attribute-Value Pairs (AVPs). These AVPs contain detailed policy parameters that define precisely which resources, privileges, and session attributes authenticated users receive. Common authorization attributes include VLAN assignment, IP address allocation, bandwidth restrictions, session timeouts, and permitted access protocols. Network devices interpret and enforce these instructions dynamically, providing precise access controls tailored to each authenticated session.

Role-based authorization policies represent a widely adopted approach for efficiently managing access permissions within RADIUS-enabled environments. Under role-based models, administrators define roles reflecting organizational structures, job functions, or specific security profiles, assigning appropriate permissions and restrictions collectively to these roles. Users assigned to these roles automatically inherit defined privileges, significantly simplifying permission management by reducing administrative overhead associated with individually assigning or modifying permissions. Role-based authorization ensures consistent security policy enforcement, rapid responsiveness to organizational changes, and clear alignment between responsibilities and access privileges.

Similarly, group-based authorization policies allow administrators to efficiently manage permissions based on user group memberships. Groups may represent departments, project teams, security clearance levels, or any collective characteristic relevant to access management. Assigning permissions to groups enables administrators to adjust privileges collectively, streamlining processes associated with organizational changes, user onboarding, or temporary assignments. Group-based authorization policies maintain consistency, efficiency, and accuracy in permission management, ensuring access privileges remain closely aligned with organizational requirements and user responsibilities.

Dynamic authorization policies further enhance network security and resource efficiency by adjusting privileges in real-time, based on contextual factors or risk assessments. Context-aware authorization evaluates multiple factors, including device security posture, geographic location, historical user behavior, and current network conditions, to determine appropriate privilege levels dynamically. For instance, authorization systems might grant broader access privileges when users connect securely from known locations using managed devices, while imposing tighter restrictions or additional authentication requirements when detecting unusual or potentially risky access patterns. Adaptive authorization policies significantly enhance security responsiveness, effectively balancing security needs against user productivity requirements.

Detailed logging, monitoring, and auditing capabilities form essential components supporting authorization policy implementation, enabling administrators to track and analyze permission usage comprehensively. Centralized authorization systems typically maintain detailed logs documenting authorization decisions, applied policy rules, resource usage, and user session attributes. Comprehensive logging facilitates critical functions, including compliance auditing, forensic analysis, security incident response, and resource optimization. Proactive monitoring and real-time analysis of authorization logs further enable administrators to detect unauthorized access attempts, policy violations, suspicious behaviors, or potential insider threats, enhancing organizational capability to respond effectively to security events.

Comprehensive lifecycle management processes ensure authorization policies remain accurate, relevant, and aligned with organizational roles and security requirements throughout user tenure. Lifecycle management practices encompass initial user provisioning, regular permission reviews, timely updates reflecting role changes or promotions, periodic recertification of permissions, and immediate de-provisioning upon employee termination or role reassignment. Regular recertification processes periodically validate authorization privileges, ensuring continuous alignment between assigned permissions and user responsibilities, significantly reducing risks associated with unauthorized access or privilege accumulation.

Integration between authorization systems, authentication solutions, and identity management platforms further streamlines authorization policy management, providing centralized control, simplified workflows, and consistent policy enforcement. Integrating centralized authorization methods like RADIUS with identity repositories such as Active Directory, LDAP directories, or HR management systems simplifies role assignment, group membership synchronization, policy definition, and permission updates. Centralized integration reduces complexity, accelerates responsiveness to organizational changes, and maintains comprehensive visibility into access and permission management across enterprise networks.

Robust authorization policy implementation also involves rigorous testing, validation, and documentation practices. Administrators must systematically verify authorization policy effectiveness, accuracy, and security alignment through comprehensive testing scenarios reflecting realistic user roles, access requirements, and potential security risks. Rigorous validation ensures correct authorization enforcement, minimizes operational disruptions, and proactively identifies potential configuration errors or unintended policy consequences. Comprehensive documentation detailing defined roles, group memberships, policy rules, applied privileges, and lifecycle management procedures further supports efficient authorization management, training, compliance verification, and security auditing processes.

User training and awareness initiatives provide essential support for effective authorization policy implementation, educating users about authorized resource usage, permissible activities, organizational expectations, and security responsibilities. Educated users better understand limitations associated with their assigned permissions, adhere more consistently to security policies, and contribute proactively to maintaining organizational security integrity. Continuous user education and communication ensure informed compliance, minimize accidental breaches resulting from misunderstandings, negligence, or permission misuse, and enhance overall organizational security posture.

Overall, implementing effective authorization policies involves comprehensive approaches encompassing centralized authorization systems, role-based or group-based permission management, dynamic and adaptive authorization techniques, rigorous monitoring practices, lifecycle management procedures, identity management integration, systematic testing, detailed documentation, and continuous user education. Organizations effectively implementing robust authorization policies significantly enhance security posture, streamline administrative processes, improve compliance capabilities, and ensure efficient, secure network resource utilization aligned precisely with organizational roles, responsibilities, and security requirements.

Session Management and Accounting

Effective session management and accounting are critical components of network administration, playing pivotal roles in maintaining security, operational efficiency, and compliance within organizational environments. While authentication and authorization primarily focus on verifying user identities and determining permitted access privileges, session management involves actively monitoring, controlling, and logging user interactions with network resources throughout their connection durations. Accounting, closely integrated with session management, refers to the systematic collection, analysis, and reporting of detailed user activity data, offering administrators comprehensive insights into network usage, resource consumption, and overall security posture. Together, these practices significantly enhance organizational capability to maintain secure, efficient network operations.

Centralized authentication systems, such as Remote Authentication Dial-In User Service (RADIUS), facilitate robust session management capabilities by enabling precise control over user sessions. Upon successful authentication and authorization, RADIUS servers issue session-specific parameters directly to network access devices through defined Attribute-Value Pairs (AVPs). These AVPs precisely dictate session characteristics such as assigned IP addresses, maximum allowable session durations, idle timeouts, bandwidth restrictions, and permitted services or applications. Network devices interpret these session parameters dynamically, enforcing policy-driven session controls tailored specifically to individual users or groups, ensuring compliance with organizational requirements and security standards.

Dynamic session management through centralized authentication enables real-time administrative control over active sessions. Administrators can enforce limitations on maximum session durations, automatically disconnect inactive sessions, or terminate connections under specific conditions, such as suspected unauthorized activity, resource overuse, or security violations. Real-time session controls significantly reduce organizational exposure to security risks associated with prolonged unattended sessions, credential compromise, or unauthorized resource access. By enforcing dynamic controls proactively, administrators minimize security vulnerabilities, improve resource utilization, and maintain precise alignment between user activities and organizational policies.

Accounting functionality, inherently integrated within centralized authentication solutions such as RADIUS, systematically captures and records comprehensive data related to user sessions, activities, and resource usage. Network access devices transmit detailed accounting packets to centralized RADIUS accounting servers, documenting session initiation and termination timestamps, total session durations, cumulative data transfers, accessed network resources, and other relevant session attributes. Centralized accounting data provides administrators valuable insights for analyzing user behaviors, detecting anomalies, planning network capacity, enforcing billing procedures, and verifying compliance with internal policies or regulatory requirements.

Detailed accounting records enable administrators to monitor network usage patterns, proactively identifying potential performance bottlenecks, resource constraints, or security vulnerabilities. Analysis of accounting data reveals insights into frequently accessed resources, peak usage periods, bandwidth consumption patterns, and emerging trends, facilitating informed decision-making regarding network optimization, resource allocation, and future infrastructure investments. Accounting data additionally serves critical functions in incident response processes, enabling administrators to reconstruct detailed user activity timelines, accurately identify involved resources, and effectively assess potential security impacts associated with suspicious activities or confirmed breaches.

Proactive monitoring and real-time analysis of session and accounting data significantly enhance organizational capability to detect and respond rapidly to potential security incidents or policy violations. Integrated monitoring solutions continuously analyze accounting logs, detecting suspicious patterns, abnormal behaviors, repeated authentication failures, or unauthorized access attempts indicative of security threats or insider misuse. Automated alerting mechanisms promptly notify administrators regarding detected anomalies, triggering immediate investigation, incident containment measures, or enforcement of additional authentication requirements. Real-time session and accounting data analysis substantially improves organizational responsiveness, reducing exposure timeframes associated with security events and minimizing potential impacts.

Lifecycle management processes encompass comprehensive practices for managing sessions effectively throughout user tenure, including provisioning initial session parameters, periodic reviews of active sessions, and timely termination upon session expiration or detected security events. Administrators regularly assess active session statuses, enforcing automatic termination of idle or prolonged connections and proactively intervening when observing deviations from expected session behaviors. Lifecycle management practices ensure continuous alignment between user sessions, organizational security standards, and operational efficiency goals, maintaining robust session management practices consistently over time.

Advanced session management techniques leverage adaptive, context-aware strategies to dynamically adjust session parameters or impose additional authentication requirements based on real-time contextual information, risk assessments, or user behavior analytics. Context-aware session controls evaluate factors such as user location, device security posture, historical behaviors, or current network conditions, adjusting session privileges dynamically or initiating supplementary verification processes when detecting elevated risk scenarios. Adaptive session management strategies effectively balance rigorous security requirements with user productivity needs, maintaining secure, efficient session management responsive precisely to evolving security conditions.

Redundant and highly available accounting infrastructures ensure continuous collection, storage, and accessibility of critical accounting data, even during primary server failures or network disruptions. Administrators commonly deploy redundant accounting servers, configured in failover pairs or load-balanced clusters, guaranteeing uninterrupted accounting capabilities essential for ongoing monitoring, security analysis, and compliance verification processes. Reliable accounting redundancy supports continuous organizational oversight, maintaining critical visibility into session activities, resource usage, and potential security incidents, even during adverse network conditions or hardware failures.

Integrating centralized session management and accounting systems with enterprise identity management solutions, directory services, or security information and event management (SIEM) platforms further streamlines administrative workflows, enhances security responsiveness, and improves compliance capabilities. Centralized integration simplifies data correlation, accelerates incident detection processes, supports automated compliance reporting, and facilitates rapid administrative interventions when addressing detected security anomalies or policy violations. Comprehensive integration enhances overall organizational efficiency, security effectiveness, and regulatory compliance posture, delivering tangible benefits across operational, security, and compliance domains.

Rigorous testing, validation, and documentation practices remain essential components supporting effective session management and accounting implementation. Administrators systematically verify proper enforcement of session controls, accurate collection and logging of accounting data, reliable operation of alerting mechanisms, and robust integration with identity management or monitoring solutions. Comprehensive documentation detailing defined session parameters, lifecycle management procedures, accounting configurations, and integration practices supports ongoing management, training, security auditing, and compliance verification processes, maintaining robust session management and accounting practices over time.

Comprehensive user education and awareness initiatives provide crucial support for effective session management and accounting practices, educating users about expected session behaviors, organizational policies regarding resource usage, security responsibilities, and potential risks associated with unauthorized or improper session activities. Educated users proactively contribute to maintaining secure, efficient network operations, adhering consistently to session parameters, and reporting suspicious activities promptly. Continuous user education reinforces informed compliance, reduces accidental breaches resulting from negligence or misunderstanding, and strengthens overall organizational security posture associated with effective session management and accounting practices.

RADIUS Accounting Records

RADIUS accounting records are fundamental components in network management and security, providing detailed, systematic documentation of user activities and session characteristics within network environments. These records are generated through the accounting functionality integrated into Remote Authentication Dial-In User Service (RADIUS), delivering critical insights into network usage patterns, resource utilization, and user behavior. Accounting records ensure comprehensive visibility into each authenticated session, facilitating proactive security management, operational optimization, resource allocation planning, and compliance verification processes. As network environments continue to expand and become increasingly complex, accurate and detailed accounting records remain essential for effective administrative oversight and network security.

The process of generating RADIUS accounting records typically initiates immediately after a successful user authentication event. Following user authentication and authorization, network access devices acting as RADIUS clients—such as wireless access points, VPN gateways, or Ethernet switches—begin transmitting accounting packets directly to centralized RADIUS accounting servers. Accounting packets are formatted consistently using RADIUS accounting packet standards, which clearly delineate session-related data points systematically organized within defined Attribute-Value Pairs (AVPs). These AVPs capture comprehensive session attributes, including session start and stop times, session duration, total data transmitted, assigned IP addresses, accessed network resources, and various other session-specific characteristics.

RADIUS accounting packets adhere strictly to a standardized packet structure, ensuring accurate and consistent interpretation across diverse network access devices and accounting servers. Each packet includes specific fields, such as packet type, identifier, authenticator, and accounting AVPs that collectively represent detailed session data. Accounting packet types include Accounting-Start, Accounting-Stop, and Accounting-Interim messages, each fulfilling specific functions in documenting ongoing session activities. Accounting-Start packets indicate session initiation, providing initial details such as user identity, network location, session parameters, and timestamps. Accounting-Stop packets document session termination events, recording final session duration, cumulative data transfer volumes, resource utilization statistics, and any session termination reasons. Interim accounting packets offer periodic updates regarding ongoing session status, continuously reporting incremental data usage, elapsed connection time, and intermediate resource consumption details.

Centralized collection and storage of RADIUS accounting records significantly streamline administrative oversight, simplifying analysis, reporting, and security monitoring processes. Accounting records maintained on centralized RADIUS accounting servers provide administrators with comprehensive, accessible documentation of network usage patterns, facilitating rapid identification of potential security anomalies, operational inefficiencies, or resource constraints. Centralized accounting databases frequently integrate seamlessly with security information and event management (SIEM) platforms, log analysis tools, or network management solutions, enabling automated correlation, real-time monitoring, and sophisticated analytical capabilities across diverse organizational security, operational, and compliance domains.

Detailed RADIUS accounting records play critical roles in proactive security management, incident detection, and forensic analysis processes. Continuous monitoring and real-time analysis of accounting logs enable administrators to detect anomalous activities, unauthorized resource access attempts, repeated authentication failures, abnormal usage patterns, or potential insider threats promptly. By analyzing accounting data systematically, administrators can quickly identify potential security incidents, initiate immediate investigative actions, reconstruct detailed timelines of user activities, accurately assess security impacts, and implement appropriate response measures effectively. Accurate accounting records provide essential forensic evidence during security investigations, enabling precise attribution, resource identification, and analysis of potential data breaches or suspicious user behaviors.

Compliance verification and regulatory auditing functions further rely extensively on accurate, detailed RADIUS accounting records. Many regulatory frameworks, including PCI DSS, HIPAA, GDPR, or industry-specific standards, mandate systematic logging, retention, and reporting of user access activities, resource utilization, and related session details. Comprehensive RADIUS accounting records enable organizations to demonstrate consistent compliance with regulatory requirements through systematic documentation of authentication attempts, resource accesses, data transfers, and user interactions within network environments. Regular compliance audits leverage detailed accounting logs to verify adherence to internal policies, regulatory standards, and security requirements, ensuring continued organizational compliance and minimizing potential legal, financial, or reputational risks associated with compliance failures.

RADIUS accounting records additionally support network operational optimization, resource allocation planning, and capacity management activities. Detailed session data provides administrators valuable insights into peak usage periods, bandwidth consumption patterns, frequently accessed resources, or emerging utilization trends. By analyzing accounting data systematically, administrators proactively identify potential performance bottlenecks, network congestion points, or resource constraints, facilitating informed decision-making regarding network infrastructure enhancements, bandwidth adjustments, or resource allocation modifications. Accurate accounting records inform capacity management practices, enabling organizations to anticipate evolving resource demands, optimize infrastructure investments, and maintain efficient, responsive network performance aligned precisely with organizational operational needs.

Redundant and highly available accounting infrastructure ensures continuous collection, retention, and accessibility of critical RADIUS accounting records, even during primary server outages, network disruptions, or hardware failures. Administrators typically deploy redundant accounting servers configured in active-passive or load-balanced clusters, ensuring uninterrupted accounting functionality essential for ongoing monitoring, security analysis, compliance verification, and operational management processes. Reliable accounting redundancy maintains continuous visibility into network session activities, resource usage patterns, and potential security events, even during adverse network conditions, hardware failures, or unexpected disruptions.

Rigorous lifecycle management processes support effective management and ongoing accuracy of RADIUS accounting records, encompassing comprehensive practices for configuring initial accounting parameters, regularly reviewing collected data, systematically archiving historical records, and securely disposing of obsolete accounting information. Regular lifecycle reviews and archival practices ensure continued relevance, accuracy, and availability of critical accounting data, supporting organizational compliance requirements, security investigations, and operational management functions consistently over time. Secure disposal practices prevent unauthorized disclosure, accidental misuse, or inappropriate retention of obsolete accounting data, maintaining regulatory compliance and information security integrity throughout accounting lifecycle processes.

Robust integration between RADIUS accounting systems, identity management solutions, directory services, or security monitoring platforms further enhances accounting data management, administrative workflows, and organizational security responsiveness. Centralized integration simplifies correlation of accounting logs with authentication records, identity repositories, network management tools, or security analysis systems, facilitating comprehensive visibility, automated monitoring, and rapid investigative actions across diverse organizational security, compliance, and operational functions. Effective integration enhances overall organizational efficiency, security effectiveness, and compliance capabilities derived directly from comprehensive RADIUS accounting records management.

Continuous administrative training, user education initiatives, and documentation practices provide essential support for effective utilization and interpretation of RADIUS accounting records, educating administrators regarding accounting configuration practices, log analysis techniques, and security incident response procedures. Comprehensive documentation detailing accounting server configurations, retention policies, lifecycle management procedures, and integration practices further supports effective administration, training, compliance verification, and security auditing functions consistently over time. Educated administrators effectively leverage comprehensive RADIUS accounting records, ensuring robust organizational security, compliance, and operational management aligned precisely with evolving network security and administrative requirements.

Integration with LDAP Directories

Integration with Lightweight Directory Access Protocol (LDAP) directories is an essential aspect of managing centralized authentication, authorization, and access control within network infrastructures. LDAP directories provide organizations with a structured, centralized repository of user information, including identities, credentials, group memberships, organizational roles, and other critical user attributes. By integrating LDAP directories with centralized authentication services, such as Remote Authentication Dial-In User Service (RADIUS), organizations significantly simplify credential management, streamline administrative workflows, enhance security consistency, and improve the overall efficiency of network access control.

LDAP directories serve as authoritative sources of user identity information, maintaining structured, hierarchical data storage that organizes user accounts, group memberships, organizational structures, and security attributes systematically. LDAP directories offer high-performance query capabilities, standardized data schemas, secure authentication mechanisms, and efficient data replication features, making them ideal solutions for managing large-scale identity repositories within enterprise environments. Integrating LDAP directories with RADIUS authentication solutions allows administrators to leverage existing identity repositories, synchronize user credentials seamlessly, enforce centralized policies consistently, and significantly reduce administrative overhead associated with managing separate user databases across network devices or authentication platforms.

When integrated with LDAP directories, RADIUS servers perform authentication and authorization tasks by directly querying LDAP identity repositories for credential verification and authorization attribute retrieval. During authentication processes, network access devices transmit user-supplied credentials to the RADIUS server, which subsequently initiates LDAP queries against the centralized directory service. LDAP queries involve securely communicating with LDAP servers using standardized protocols, securely verifying credentials, retrieving user group memberships, confirming authorization privileges, and determining assigned network access parameters. Based on information retrieved directly from LDAP directories, RADIUS servers authorize user access dynamically, specifying appropriate session attributes, VLAN assignments, bandwidth restrictions, IP address allocations, or other network parameters defined within centralized identity repositories.

Implementing LDAP integration with RADIUS authentication requires careful consideration regarding secure communication channels, directory schema designs, attribute mappings, performance optimization, and access controls. Secure communication between RADIUS servers and LDAP directories typically leverages encrypted Transport Layer Security (TLS) connections, ensuring confidentiality and integrity of credential verification exchanges, attribute retrieval operations, and directory queries transmitted across network environments. Strong encryption methods and secure LDAP (LDAPS) implementations significantly mitigate risks associated with credential interception, unauthorized access, or potential man-in-the-middle attacks targeting authentication transactions between RADIUS servers and centralized LDAP repositories.

Directory schema designs within LDAP integration scenarios require precise definition of data structures, attribute mappings, and organizational hierarchy layouts facilitating efficient authentication queries, authorization lookups, and data synchronization processes between RADIUS servers and LDAP directories. Administrators must carefully design directory schemas accommodating RADIUS authentication requirements, ensuring accurate attribute mappings aligning precisely with expected credential verification inputs, authorization attribute formats, and session parameter definitions used during network access control transactions. Clearly defined schemas, consistent attribute mappings, and standardized data structures significantly enhance LDAP integration reliability, authentication accuracy, authorization efficiency, and overall directory performance within RADIUS authentication processes.

Attribute mapping configurations remain critical components supporting effective LDAP integration, translating attribute names, formats, and data types accurately between LDAP directory schemas and RADIUS authentication attribute requirements. Administrators configure precise mappings associating LDAP user attributes with

RADIUS attribute definitions, ensuring correct interpretation, accurate credential verification, efficient authorization lookups, and seamless communication between centralized identity repositories and network authentication systems. Effective attribute mappings simplify administrative workflows, streamline credential management processes, enhance policy consistency, and improve security reliability within integrated LDAP-RADIUS environments.

Performance optimization considerations are crucial aspects during LDAP integration implementations, ensuring rapid authentication queries, efficient directory lookups, and responsive authorization attribute retrieval operations, particularly within large-scale environments involving extensive identity repositories or high-volume authentication transactions. Administrators employ various performance optimization techniques, including indexing frequently queried directory attributes, efficiently structuring directory hierarchies, configuring replication for load distribution, optimizing LDAP connection pooling configurations, and tuning query mechanisms employed during authentication processes. Rigorous performance optimization practices significantly enhance responsiveness, reliability, and scalability of LDAP integration solutions, ensuring consistently efficient authentication operations, rapid authorization attribute retrieval, and minimal latency impacts during RADIUS authentication transactions.

Access control configurations further ensure secure, controlled interactions between RADIUS authentication services and centralized LDAP directory repositories, restricting query permissions strictly to necessary directory objects, attributes, and organizational hierarchies essential for authentication and authorization tasks. Administrators configure detailed access control rules within LDAP directories, limiting RADIUS server privileges specifically to read-only queries targeting credential verification attributes, user identities, group memberships, and defined authorization parameters. Robust access control mechanisms prevent unauthorized disclosure, accidental modification, or malicious misuse of sensitive directory data, maintaining directory security integrity throughout LDAP integration processes supporting RADIUS authentication services.

Comprehensive monitoring, logging, and auditing capabilities provide critical support for LDAP integration solutions, enabling administrators to track authentication queries, authorization attribute lookups, directory connection statuses, transaction response times, and overall integration performance systematically. Integrated monitoring solutions continuously analyze LDAP integration operations, detecting query failures, latency issues, attribute retrieval errors, or suspicious query patterns indicative of potential configuration problems, performance bottlenecks, or unauthorized access attempts targeting centralized identity repositories. Proactive monitoring, detailed logging, and regular auditing practices significantly improve LDAP integration reliability, responsiveness, and security, enabling administrators to identify, investigate, and resolve potential issues promptly, minimizing operational disruptions, authentication failures, or security vulnerabilities arising within integrated LDAP-RADIUS environments.

Lifecycle management practices support ongoing LDAP integration effectiveness, encompassing comprehensive procedures for configuring initial LDAP-RADIUS integration settings, periodically reviewing attribute mappings, regularly updating directory schemas, systematically maintaining attribute consistency, and promptly addressing evolving integration requirements arising from organizational changes, directory updates, or authentication policy adjustments. Lifecycle management ensures continued accuracy, reliability, and efficiency of LDAP integration solutions, maintaining robust authentication capabilities consistently over time despite organizational evolution, directory expansions, or evolving authentication needs.

Systematic documentation detailing LDAP-RADIUS integration configurations, attribute mappings, schema definitions, access control policies, performance optimization practices, and monitoring strategies provides essential support for effective integration management, administrator training, compliance auditing, and security incident response procedures consistently over time. Comprehensive documentation ensures continued integration reliability, facilitates efficient troubleshooting processes, supports compliance verification requirements, and enables consistent application of best practices across integrated LDAP-RADIUS environments.

Administrator training and continuous education initiatives further enhance LDAP integration effectiveness, educating administrative personnel regarding directory schema design considerations, secure LDAP connection methods, attribute mapping techniques, performance optimization strategies, access control configurations, and proactive monitoring practices associated with integrated LDAP-RADIUS authentication solutions. Educated administrators effectively leverage comprehensive LDAP directory integration capabilities, maintaining robust, secure, efficient authentication processes aligned precisely with organizational security requirements, compliance standards, and operational needs.

Active Directory and RADIUS

The integration of Active Directory (AD) with RADIUS is a critical component in modern network environments that require centralized authentication, authorization, and accounting for users and devices. Active Directory, developed by Microsoft, is the dominant directory service used in enterprise networks. It stores user identities, group memberships, organizational units, and security policies, providing a single source of truth for managing user access and permissions across multiple systems and applications. When paired with RADIUS, a widely used AAA protocol, organizations can leverage their existing AD infrastructure to authenticate users attempting to access network resources through VPNs, Wi-Fi, wired networks, and other remote access services.

The relationship between Active Directory and RADIUS is built on the premise that organizations need a seamless method to verify user credentials against a centralized directory before granting access to critical resources. RADIUS servers, such as FreeRADIUS or Microsoft NPS (Network Policy Server), are configured to act as intermediaries between the access client (such as a VPN client or a wireless device) and the Active Directory domain controller. When a user attempts to authenticate, the Network Access Server (NAS) forwards the authentication request to the RADIUS server. The RADIUS server then validates the credentials by querying Active Directory, typically using protocols such as LDAP or Kerberos, depending on the RADIUS implementation and configuration.

A typical deployment scenario involves configuring the RADIUS server to operate as a domain member, allowing it to authenticate users directly against the Active Directory domain. This configuration enables the RADIUS server to take advantage of the security mechanisms and policies enforced within the AD environment, such as password complexity rules, account lockout policies, and group-based access control. By integrating RADIUS with Active Directory, organizations can enforce consistent authentication policies across disparate network access technologies, including wireless LANs secured with WPA2-Enterprise or WPA3-Enterprise, VPN concentrators, and wired 802.1X-enabled switches.

An important aspect of this integration is the support for various authentication protocols. The RADIUS server can process authentication requests using protocols like PAP, CHAP, MS-CHAPv2, or EAP methods such as EAP-TLS and PEAP. These protocols are often selected based on the security requirements of the organization and the capabilities of the client devices. For instance, EAP-TLS is favored in environments where mutual certificate-based authentication is required, while PEAP-MSCHAPv2 is commonly used for username and password-based authentication secured within an encrypted tunnel.

Microsoft NPS is one of the most widely used RADIUS servers when integrating with Active Directory. As a role within Windows Server, NPS simplifies the process of connecting RADIUS to AD. It provides a native interface to create and enforce network policies, define conditions and constraints for access requests, and log accounting data. Administrators can use NPS to define granular access controls based on AD group memberships, user attributes, or device characteristics. This level of control ensures that only authorized users and devices can access specific network segments or resources, which is especially crucial in enterprise networks with segmented architectures and strict compliance requirements.

In addition to authentication, RADIUS in conjunction with Active Directory enables dynamic authorization. This means that access decisions can be made not only based on the user's credentials but also on contextual factors such as the time of day, client IP address, or the location of the access attempt. For example, an organization may permit remote VPN access to certain users only during business hours or from predefined geographical locations. These policies can be enforced within NPS or another RADIUS server integrated with AD, providing an additional layer of security and compliance enforcement.

Another benefit of integrating Active Directory with RADIUS is centralized auditing and reporting. When RADIUS logs are combined with Active Directory's event logs, administrators gain a comprehensive view of authentication activities across the entire network. This centralized logging is valuable for forensic investigations, compliance audits, and ongoing security monitoring. Administrators can quickly identify failed login attempts, unauthorized access attempts, or patterns indicative of brute-force attacks.

Organizations also benefit from the scalability of this integration. Large enterprises can deploy multiple RADIUS servers in a redundant and load-balanced configuration, ensuring high availability and reliable performance during peak authentication loads. Each RADIUS server can query the same Active Directory domain or trusted domains within a forest, supporting geographically distributed networks and branch offices. Additionally, multi-domain environments are supported through RADIUS referrals or by deploying RADIUS servers in each domain with appropriate trust relationships configured in AD.

Security considerations are paramount when integrating RADIUS with Active Directory. To protect the credentials exchanged during the authentication process, administrators should configure the RADIUS server to require secure authentication protocols and encrypt RADIUS traffic using IPsec or Transport Layer Security (TLS). This prevents sensitive information, such as usernames and passwords, from being exposed during transmission over potentially insecure networks. Furthermore, securing the communication channel between the RADIUS server and the Active Directory domain controller is essential, often achieved by enforcing LDAP over SSL (LDAPS) or leveraging Kerberos tickets for authentication.

Modern trends also involve combining this integration with multi-factor authentication (MFA) solutions. By layering MFA on top of RADIUS authentication against Active Directory, organizations significantly enhance their security posture. Users may be required to provide a second factor, such as a time-based one-time password (TOTP), a hardware token, or a push notification response, before gaining access to network resources. This approach mitigates risks associated with compromised passwords, which remain a leading cause of security breaches.

Ultimately, integrating Active Directory with RADIUS creates a robust and flexible foundation for managing network access in a secure and scalable manner. It allows organizations to unify user management, enforce granular access controls, and maintain compliance with regulatory standards, all while leveraging existing AD investments. As organizations continue to adopt hybrid and cloud environments, this integration will remain a cornerstone of secure network authentication strategies.

SQL Databases and RADIUS Integration

Integrating SQL databases with RADIUS servers is a common practice in organizations seeking to enhance scalability, flexibility, and manageability of user authentication and accounting processes. By leveraging the structured and query-driven nature of SQL databases, administrators can centralize and streamline the storage and retrieval of user credentials, session data, and accounting information. This integration enables RADIUS servers to interact with relational databases such as MySQL, PostgreSQL, Microsoft SQL Server, or Oracle, providing a powerful backend to support dynamic user access control policies, detailed reporting, and custom business logic.

At the core of this integration is the ability of the RADIUS server to offload authentication and accounting tasks to the SQL database. Instead of maintaining static user entries in flat files or local configurations, the RADIUS server queries the SQL database in real time during each authentication request. When a user attempts to connect to the network through a VPN, Wi-Fi, or wired 802.1X infrastructure, the Network Access Server (NAS) forwards the request to the RADIUS server. The RADIUS server then performs SQL queries against the database to verify user credentials, retrieve user profiles, or log session details. This dynamic approach offers significant advantages, particularly for service providers and large enterprises that manage a high volume of users and frequent changes to user accounts.

One of the most common scenarios is storing user authentication information, such as usernames, hashed passwords, and group memberships, in the SQL database. The RADIUS server can be configured to execute SQL queries that validate the credentials provided by the user against the records stored in the database. Passwords are typically stored using secure hashing algorithms, such as bcrypt, SHA-256, or PBKDF2, to prevent plaintext exposure and enhance security. The flexibility of SQL allows administrators to design custom schemas that align with their specific business requirements, incorporating additional fields such as expiration dates, account status, or user-specific policies.

Beyond authentication, SQL databases play a pivotal role in RADIUS accounting. The RADIUS server records session start and stop times, data usage, session durations, and other accounting details into SQL tables. This information is vital for organizations that require accurate usage records for billing, compliance, or auditing purposes. Internet Service Providers (ISPs), for instance, rely heavily on SQL-backed RADIUS accounting to generate invoices based on user consumption patterns, while enterprises use it to monitor employee network activity and ensure adherence to acceptable use policies. SQL databases also support complex queries and reporting capabilities, enabling administrators to extract meaningful insights from accounting data through tools such as SQL joins, aggregate functions, and advanced filtering.

A key benefit of integrating RADIUS with SQL databases is the ability to implement dynamic authorization policies. By storing user roles, access levels, or other attributes in SQL tables, the RADIUS server can apply logic during the authentication process to determine the appropriate level of access for each user. For example, a user belonging to a VIP customer group might receive a higher bandwidth allocation or access to premium network services, while standard users are assigned default restrictions. This level of granularity is achieved by configuring the RADIUS server to retrieve specific attributes from the SQL database and include them in the Access-Accept packet sent back to the NAS.

Additionally, SQL databases enable seamless integration with external systems and applications. Many organizations maintain user information in customer relationship management (CRM) systems, enterprise resource planning (ERP) platforms, or other databases. By synchronizing or linking these systems to the SQL database used by the RADIUS server, organizations can create a unified identity management ecosystem. This integration reduces administrative overhead, as updates to user information made in external systems can automatically reflect in the RADIUS authentication flow without requiring manual intervention.

Performance and scalability are also significantly enhanced through SQL integration. SQL databases are optimized to handle large volumes of transactions with high availability and reliability. Organizations can deploy SQL clusters or replication strategies to ensure database resilience and load balancing, supporting thousands or even millions of concurrent RADIUS transactions. Additionally, the use of database indexing and query optimization techniques further improves the response time of authentication and accounting queries, which is crucial in environments with strict service-level agreements (SLAs) or high user concurrency.

The integration process between RADIUS and SQL databases typically involves configuring database connection parameters, defining SQL queries for authentication, authorization, and accounting, and setting up appropriate user privileges on the database server. Popular RADIUS servers like FreeRADIUS offer native SQL modules that simplify this integration. Administrators can configure SQL-related directives in the RADIUS server's configuration files to control how queries are executed and how results are processed. These configurations often include placeholders for dynamic query generation, allowing the RADIUS server to pass user-provided values, such as usernames or NAS IP addresses, directly into the SQL queries.

Security considerations are critical when deploying SQL-backed RADIUS systems. Secure communication between the RADIUS server and the SQL database must be enforced using transport encryption mechanisms like TLS or SSL. Database credentials should be stored securely within the RADIUS server and access to the database should be restricted to only trusted hosts and services. Additionally, SQL injection protections must be in place, either through the use of parameterized queries or prepared statements, to prevent malicious users from exploiting vulnerabilities in the query logic.

Modern deployments also increasingly involve cloud-based SQL databases, offering elastic scalability and managed services. Cloud-native RADIUS implementations often leverage databases hosted in platforms like Amazon RDS, Google Cloud SQL, or Azure SQL Database, benefiting from automatic backups, failover capabilities, and reduced infrastructure management. These solutions are particularly attractive to organizations adopting hybrid or fully cloud-based network architectures, allowing them to extend RADIUS authentication and accounting capabilities beyond traditional on-premises environments.

Overall, integrating SQL databases with RADIUS unlocks a new dimension of control, automation, and efficiency in managing network access and user activities. By coupling the robustness of relational databases with the versatility of the RADIUS protocol, organizations gain a powerful and scalable solution capable of meeting diverse security, business, and operational requirements.

Redundancy and High Availability

Redundancy and high availability are essential concepts when designing and deploying RADIUS servers in enterprise and service provider networks. As RADIUS plays a critical role in managing authentication, authorization, and accounting for network access, any failure or downtime in the RADIUS infrastructure can result in service disruptions, denied access for legitimate users, and a significant impact on business operations. Ensuring that RADIUS services remain available and resilient under all circumstances requires a thoughtful strategy that incorporates multiple layers of redundancy and fault tolerance.

At its core, redundancy in a RADIUS environment refers to the deployment of multiple RADIUS servers that work together to provide continuous service availability. These servers are typically deployed in active-active or active-passive configurations, depending on the organization's specific requirements and preferences. In an active-active setup, multiple RADIUS servers operate simultaneously, handling authentication and accounting requests in parallel. This load-sharing approach not only enhances performance by distributing the processing load across several servers but also ensures that if one server fails, the others continue to handle requests without service interruption. In an active-passive configuration, a primary server handles all incoming requests under normal circumstances, while one or more secondary servers stand by to take over automatically if the primary server becomes unavailable.

The configuration of redundancy begins at the Network Access Server (NAS) level, where multiple RADIUS servers can be defined. Most NAS devices, including VPN concentrators, wireless controllers, and 802.1X-enabled switches, support the specification of a primary RADIUS server along with one or more secondary servers. When the primary server fails to respond within a predefined timeout period, the NAS automatically reroutes authentication requests to the next available server in the list. This failover mechanism is crucial in ensuring continuous access for users even in the event of server outages, maintenance windows, or network disruptions affecting the primary RADIUS instance.

To further enhance high availability, organizations often distribute redundant RADIUS servers across multiple physical locations or data centers. Geographical redundancy protects against site-specific failures, such as power outages, natural disasters, or connectivity issues affecting a single location. By placing RADIUS servers in diverse regions or zones, the risk of a single point of failure is greatly reduced. This approach is particularly important for large enterprises and service providers operating in multiple regions or countries, as it guarantees that users in different locations can always authenticate against a nearby, operational RADIUS server.

In addition to deploying multiple servers, high availability also depends on the use of reliable and redundant network infrastructure. The RADIUS servers themselves must be connected to the network through redundant links, switches, and routers, ensuring that network hardware failures do not isolate the servers from the NAS devices or the backend identity sources such as LDAP, Active Directory, or SQL databases. Network redundancy is typically achieved through technologies like link aggregation, spanning tree protocols, dynamic routing, and redundant paths between network nodes.

Beyond the network layer, database redundancy is another critical component of a highly available RADIUS system. Many RADIUS servers rely on external databases to retrieve user credentials, group memberships, or to store accounting data. Implementing database clustering or replication ensures that the failure of a single database server does not interrupt RADIUS operations. SQL clusters, master-slave replication setups, and distributed database architectures allow RADIUS servers to continue querying or logging data even if one or more database nodes experience issues.

Load balancing is a key strategy for both redundancy and performance optimization in RADIUS deployments. Load balancers, whether hardware-based or software-based, distribute incoming authentication and accounting requests evenly across multiple RADIUS servers. This prevents individual servers from becoming overloaded and ensures that resources are efficiently utilized. Load balancers also provide health checks and monitoring, automatically rerouting traffic away from servers that are unresponsive or underperforming. Some organizations use DNS round-robin techniques for basic load balancing, while others implement more sophisticated solutions with advanced traffic management and failover capabilities.

Session state replication between RADIUS servers is an advanced technique used in high-availability environments where maintaining session continuity is critical. In scenarios where users authenticate against one RADIUS server and that server subsequently becomes unavailable, session replication allows another RADIUS server to take over the session without forcing the user to reauthenticate. This is especially useful in large wireless networks where roaming users may move between access points or controllers relying on different RADIUS servers. Session state replication reduces disruptions and enhances the user experience by maintaining uninterrupted network access.

Monitoring and proactive maintenance are essential components of a successful redundancy and high-availability strategy. Administrators must implement robust monitoring tools that provide real-time visibility into the health and performance of RADIUS servers, network infrastructure, and associated databases. Alerts should be configured to notify administrators of any anomalies, such as server failures, degraded performance, or excessive response times. Proactive monitoring enables rapid identification and resolution of issues before they escalate into service outages.

Configuration synchronization between redundant RADIUS servers is another important factor. Consistency in server configurations, including authentication policies, client definitions, logging parameters, and security settings, ensures that failover processes do not result in different behaviors or unexpected access denials. Automated configuration management tools, version control systems, or manual procedures should be used to maintain identical configurations across all RADIUS servers within the redundant environment.

Security considerations are tightly integrated with high-availability planning. Redundant servers must be equally secured with strong authentication protocols, encrypted communications, and hardened operating systems to prevent attackers from exploiting backup systems as points of entry. High-availability configurations should also account for distributed denial-of-service (DDoS) mitigation measures, ensuring that the RADIUS infrastructure remains resilient against malicious attacks designed to overwhelm authentication services.

As networks evolve and organizations adopt hybrid and cloud-based architectures, RADIUS redundancy strategies are expanding to include cloud-based RADIUS services or hybrid models that combine on-premises and cloud-hosted RADIUS servers. Cloud RADIUS services offer built-in redundancy and geographical distribution, reducing the burden of managing physical infrastructure while maintaining high availability. These services can be integrated with on-premises environments to provide additional failover capacity or to extend authentication services to remote locations and cloud-hosted applications.

The implementation of redundancy and high availability in RADIUS deployments is not a one-size-fits-all solution. Each organization must assess its specific network topology, business requirements, and risk tolerance to design a redundancy strategy that meets its needs. Whether through simple primary-secondary failover configurations or complex multi-site, load-balanced architectures with session replication, the ultimate goal is to ensure that authentication and accounting services remain continuously available, reliable, and secure.

Load Balancing Techniques

Load balancing techniques play a pivotal role in ensuring the reliability, scalability, and optimal performance of RADIUS infrastructures, especially in enterprise and service provider environments where large volumes of authentication, authorization, and accounting requests are processed around the clock. By distributing incoming traffic evenly across multiple RADIUS servers, load balancing prevents individual servers from becoming overwhelmed and helps maintain low latency, high throughput, and continuous availability of authentication services.

One of the most common approaches to load balancing in RADIUS environments is DNS-based load distribution, commonly referred to as DNS round-robin. In this method, multiple IP addresses corresponding to different RADIUS servers are registered under a single DNS name. When a NAS or client queries the DNS for the RADIUS server's IP address, it receives a list of IP addresses, typically rotated in order to balance the load. While this method is simple and easy to implement, it lacks intelligence in handling server health and performance. DNS servers are not aware of whether a particular RADIUS server is functioning correctly or overloaded. As a result, DNS round-robin is often combined with other monitoring techniques or used in non-critical scenarios where basic distribution is sufficient.

More advanced and efficient load balancing is achieved through the deployment of dedicated hardware or software-based load balancers that sit in front of the RADIUS servers. These devices or services act as intermediaries, accepting incoming RADIUS requests and intelligently distributing them to the backend servers based on predefined algorithms and real-time server health checks. Hardware appliances from vendors like F5, Citrix, or A10 Networks, and software-based solutions such as HAProxy or NGINX, are widely used in production environments to implement this layer of traffic management.

Load balancers typically offer several algorithms for distributing traffic, each with specific advantages depending on the operational goals. One of the most commonly used is the round-robin algorithm, where requests are distributed sequentially to each RADIUS server in the pool. This method is effective when all backend servers have similar capacities and performance characteristics. However, in environments where RADIUS servers may differ in hardware specifications, load, or geographical location, a weighted round-robin approach can be used. Weighted round-robin assigns more traffic to higher-capacity servers by giving them a larger share of incoming requests.

Another frequently used method is least connections, where the load balancer directs incoming requests to the server currently handling the fewest active sessions. This dynamic algorithm helps prevent imbalances that could occur if one server ends up processing more complex or longer-running sessions than others. Least connections is particularly useful in RADIUS environments where session duration and resource consumption can vary significantly between users and access methods, such as VPN users consuming more processing power than simple wireless LAN users.

Geographical load balancing, or Global Server Load Balancing (GSLB), is often implemented by organizations with distributed data centers or multi-region architectures. In this scenario, load balancers take into account the physical location of the NAS or client requesting authentication and direct the traffic to the nearest or most appropriate RADIUS server. By doing so, latency is reduced, and the overall user experience is improved. GSLB can be further enhanced by incorporating health checks and server metrics to ensure that requests are always directed to servers that are not only geographically optimal but also fully operational and under acceptable load levels.

A key feature of modern load balancing solutions is the ability to perform deep health checks on backend RADIUS servers. Simple ping or TCP port checks are often insufficient, as they may indicate that a server is reachable even if the RADIUS service itself is malfunctioning. Advanced load balancers can be configured to send actual RADIUS Access-Request packets to backend servers and validate the received responses. Only servers that respond appropriately and within acceptable response times are considered healthy and eligible to receive production traffic. This proactive health monitoring is vital to ensure that authentication requests are not sent to servers experiencing issues or degraded performance.

Session persistence, sometimes referred to as sticky sessions, is another consideration in RADIUS load balancing. In some cases, particularly with EAP-based authentication methods like EAP-TLS or PEAP, it is desirable for a user session to be consistently handled by the same RADIUS server for the duration of the authentication process. Load balancers can be configured to track session identifiers or source IP addresses to maintain session persistence, ensuring that the flow of authentication messages between the client, NAS, and RADIUS server remains uninterrupted and consistent.

Load balancing also plays a crucial role in supporting redundancy and failover strategies. By integrating load balancers with high-availability architectures, organizations can ensure that if a RADIUS server fails or is taken offline for maintenance, incoming requests are automatically rerouted to available servers without affecting users. Load balancers can work in concert with redundancy mechanisms at the network and database levels to provide a seamless and resilient authentication experience.

In cloud-native environments, load balancing extends to virtualized and containerized RADIUS instances. Organizations leveraging public or private clouds can use built-in cloud load balancers such as AWS Elastic Load Balancing, Azure Load Balancer, or Google Cloud Load Balancer to distribute RADIUS traffic across virtual machines or containers running RADIUS services. These cloud-native solutions offer auto-scaling capabilities, automatically adding or removing backend RADIUS instances based on traffic patterns and server resource utilization, thus providing elasticity and cost efficiency.

Additionally, software-defined networking (SDN) and network function virtualization (NFV) are emerging technologies that further enhance load balancing techniques for RADIUS. SDN allows administrators to dynamically adjust network traffic flows and policies, including the distribution of authentication requests, while NFV enables the deployment of RADIUS servers and load balancers as virtualized network functions that can be orchestrated and scaled programmatically.

Security is a vital consideration when designing load balancing architectures for RADIUS. The load balancer itself becomes a critical component in the authentication infrastructure and must be secured accordingly. This includes implementing strong access controls, encrypting management interfaces, and hardening the underlying operating system or appliance. Furthermore, load balancers should support encrypted RADIUS traffic, such as RADIUS over TLS or IPsec tunnels, ensuring that sensitive authentication data remains protected throughout the entire flow from the NAS to the backend servers.

Ultimately, the choice of load balancing technique depends on the specific needs of the organization, including performance expectations, geographical distribution, redundancy requirements, and security policies. Whether using simple round-robin DNS configurations, dedicated load balancer appliances, cloud-native solutions, or a combination of methods, effective load balancing is essential for delivering a scalable, resilient, and high-performing RADIUS infrastructure. The successful implementation of these techniques helps ensure that authentication services remain responsive and available, even under the most demanding network conditions.

RADIUS Proxy Servers

RADIUS proxy servers serve as intermediaries between Network Access Servers (NAS) and one or more backend RADIUS servers, forwarding authentication, authorization, and accounting requests based on specific routing rules or business logic. The use of RADIUS proxies is a common practice in complex network environments where organizations need to route requests to different authentication domains, support multi-tenant architectures, or integrate with external service providers. By introducing a proxy layer into the RADIUS infrastructure, administrators gain more flexibility and control over how authentication traffic is handled and distributed across the network.

A primary reason for deploying RADIUS proxy servers is to support roaming scenarios. In environments where users from multiple organizations or service providers require access to shared network infrastructure, such as in eduroam or wireless roaming federations, a RADIUS proxy is essential. When a NAS receives an authentication request from a user belonging to an external domain, it forwards the request to the local RADIUS proxy server. The proxy inspects attributes such as the realm or domain portion of the username (e.g., user@example.com) and uses preconfigured routing rules to direct the request to the appropriate home RADIUS server responsible for that domain. This forwarding process ensures that authentication decisions are made by the user's home organization, which has authority over their credentials and access rights.

RADIUS proxies are also widely used in multi-tenant networks, such as those operated by managed service providers (MSPs) or large enterprises with multiple subsidiaries or business units. In these environments, a single shared NAS infrastructure may serve users from multiple independent organizations, each maintaining its own RADIUS server. The proxy server functions as a central traffic director, routing requests to the correct backend system based on the identity of the user or other attributes included in the RADIUS request. This approach allows the service provider to offer a unified network access experience while ensuring that each organization retains control over its own authentication policies and user database.

Another critical use case for RADIUS proxies is to offload or distribute traffic in large-scale deployments. In high-demand environments, direct communication between NAS devices and backend RADIUS servers may lead to bottlenecks or uneven load distribution. By introducing a proxy layer, organizations can centralize the handling of incoming requests, apply load-balancing algorithms, and distribute traffic evenly across multiple backend servers. Proxies can integrate with load-balancing solutions or implement their own internal load distribution logic, reducing the risk of server overload and improving the overall responsiveness of the authentication system.

RADIUS proxies are also instrumental in supporting policy enforcement at the edge of the network. Before forwarding a request to the home RADIUS server, a proxy may apply additional filtering, modification, or inspection of RADIUS attributes to ensure that the request complies with predefined security or business policies. For example, a proxy may reject requests originating from unauthorized NAS devices, sanitize attribute values, or add additional attributes such as VLAN assignment or session timeout settings based on the organization's policies. This pre-processing capability allows administrators to enforce consistent security and compliance measures across different NAS devices and network segments.

One of the most common configurations in RADIUS proxy scenarios is realm-based routing. The proxy server inspects the realm suffix of the username to determine where to forward the request. For example, requests for users in the domain @branch1.com may be routed to one RADIUS server, while requests for @branch2.com are directed to a different server. In more advanced setups, routing decisions may be based on multiple factors, including the NAS IP address, called station ID, or other RADIUS attributes. This flexibility allows organizations to implement highly customized and granular routing logic tailored to their network architecture and business needs.

Security considerations are paramount when deploying RADIUS proxies, as they introduce additional points of communication within the authentication flow. All RADIUS traffic between NAS devices, proxies, and backend servers should be encrypted and authenticated using shared secrets or more advanced mechanisms such as RADIUS over TLS (RadSec) or IPsec tunnels. Protecting the integrity and confidentiality of authentication data is essential to prevent unauthorized access, man-in-the-middle attacks, or data leakage. Additionally, the proxy itself should be hardened and monitored to ensure that it does not become a point of vulnerability within the infrastructure.

RADIUS proxies also support accounting request forwarding, ensuring that session and usage data collected by the NAS reaches the appropriate accounting servers. This is especially important in service provider environments where billing or usage reporting is handled by the user's home organization. Proxies can aggregate, filter, or even transform accounting data before forwarding it, ensuring compatibility with diverse backend systems or regulatory reporting requirements.

Scalability is another advantage provided by RADIUS proxy servers. By decoupling the NAS devices from the backend RADIUS servers, proxies enable organizations to expand their infrastructure more easily. Additional backend servers can be added without requiring configuration changes on each individual NAS. Instead, the proxy serves as the central point of configuration and routing, simplifying management and reducing operational overhead. In geographically distributed networks, proxies can be deployed in regional data centers, improving latency and redundancy by directing requests to the nearest available backend server.

Some RADIUS proxy implementations also provide advanced features such as session correlation, dynamic attribute manipulation, or integration with external systems via APIs. For instance, a proxy could interface with a central policy engine or identity management platform to make real-time access decisions based on contextual data, such as user risk scores or device posture. This level of integration enhances security by incorporating additional layers of intelligence into the authentication process.

RADIUS proxies are supported by many open-source and commercial RADIUS solutions, with FreeRADIUS being one of the most popular choices. FreeRADIUS offers robust proxy capabilities out of the box, allowing administrators to define proxy realms, home servers, load-balancing pools, and failover mechanisms through straightforward configuration files. Commercial RADIUS appliances often provide graphical user interfaces and additional automation features to simplify the deployment and management of proxy functionality.

Ultimately, RADIUS proxy servers are a versatile and powerful component of modern AAA architectures. Whether used to support roaming federations, enable multi-tenant access control, enhance scalability, or enforce policy compliance, proxies offer the flexibility and control needed to manage complex authentication ecosystems. By intelligently routing and managing RADIUS traffic, proxies ensure that authentication services remain resilient, secure, and aligned with the dynamic requirements of modern networks.

Securing RADIUS Communications

Securing RADIUS communications is one of the most important tasks for network administrators and security teams when designing and maintaining authentication infrastructures. RADIUS is a widely used protocol for managing user access, but in its default form, it has significant security limitations. Originally designed in an era when many networks were isolated and internal, RADIUS transmits sensitive information such as usernames, passwords, and session attributes without encrypting the entire payload. While it does apply hashing to the password field using a shared secret and MD5, this level of protection is no longer considered sufficient in modern security contexts. For these reasons, implementing additional layers of security is crucial to protect the confidentiality, integrity, and authenticity of RADIUS communications across the network.

The first and most common method to secure RADIUS traffic is through the use of shared secrets between RADIUS clients (such as NAS devices) and RADIUS servers. These shared secrets act as symmetric keys used to hash certain parts of the RADIUS packet, including the password attribute. While shared secrets provide a basic layer of integrity and password obfuscation, they do not encrypt the entire packet or prevent traffic analysis. Moreover, when weak shared secrets are used or when secrets are reused across multiple clients and servers, the risk of brute-force attacks and credential compromise increases. As a best practice, shared secrets should be complex, unique per client, and stored securely to minimize exposure.

To address the limitations of basic shared secret mechanisms, organizations increasingly adopt RADIUS over Transport Layer Security (TLS), commonly referred to as RadSec. RadSec encapsulates RADIUS packets within a TLS session, providing full encryption and mutual authentication between RADIUS servers and clients. This approach ensures that all attributes, including those not hashed in standard RADIUS (such as usernames or accounting data), are fully protected from eavesdropping and tampering. RadSec is particularly recommended for scenarios where RADIUS traffic traverses untrusted or public networks, such as when implementing federated authentication systems or when RADIUS proxies communicate across wide-area networks (WANs) or the internet.

RadSec relies on the use of X.509 certificates for server and client authentication. Both RADIUS servers and clients must possess valid digital certificates signed by a trusted Certificate Authority (CA). Mutual TLS (mTLS) is established before any RADIUS traffic is exchanged, ensuring that both parties are verified and trusted. The process of deploying RadSec involves generating private keys and certificate signing requests (CSRs) for each participating system, obtaining certificates from a CA, and configuring the RADIUS software to enforce TLS on all communication channels. Administrators must also carefully manage certificate lifecycles, including renewals, revocations, and periodic audits to prevent lapses in security coverage.

Another option to secure RADIUS communications is the use of IPsec tunnels between RADIUS clients and servers. IPsec operates at the network layer and can encrypt all traffic between endpoints, including RADIUS packets. IPsec provides both encryption and authentication through mechanisms such as Encapsulating Security Payload (ESP) and Authentication Header (AH). This method is commonly employed in environments where administrators seek to secure multiple types of traffic beyond RADIUS, or when integrating with existing VPN infrastructures. While effective, IPsec typically involves more complex configuration and maintenance compared to RadSec, as it requires coordination with network teams and may be subject to additional routing and firewall considerations.

In addition to transport-level security, RADIUS servers themselves must be hardened to mitigate potential threats. This includes limiting access to the RADIUS service to only trusted IP addresses or subnets, typically through firewall rules or access control lists (ACLs). Open or misconfigured RADIUS servers exposed to the internet can be exploited for various attacks, including amplification in distributed denial-of-service (DDoS) campaigns. Ensuring that RADIUS servers only accept requests from authorized NAS devices and proxies significantly reduces the attack surface and helps protect the infrastructure from abuse.

Logging and monitoring of RADIUS communications are essential to detect and respond to potential security incidents. Administrators should configure RADIUS servers to generate detailed logs of authentication attempts, including timestamps, client IP addresses, usernames, and authentication outcomes. These logs can be integrated with centralized security information and event management (SIEM) platforms to enable real-time analysis and alerting. Unusual patterns, such as repeated failed login attempts, access attempts from unauthorized devices, or unexpected traffic spikes, may indicate malicious activity that requires immediate investigation.

To further enhance the security of RADIUS communications, organizations should enforce the use of strong authentication methods. While RADIUS supports legacy protocols like PAP and CHAP, these methods are vulnerable to interception and replay attacks. Modern deployments should favor more secure protocols such as EAP-TLS or PEAP, which encapsulate user credentials within encrypted tunnels or utilize certificates for mutual authentication. By combining secure transport with robust authentication protocols, organizations create a layered defense against both external and internal threats.

Configuration management is another critical aspect of securing RADIUS communications. All configuration files, including those defining shared secrets, TLS settings, or client definitions, should be stored securely with appropriate file permissions. Changes to RADIUS configurations should follow established change control processes to prevent unauthorized modifications and ensure consistency across redundant or distributed RADIUS servers. Configuration files should also be regularly reviewed to identify potential misconfigurations, deprecated protocols, or obsolete entries that could introduce vulnerabilities.

Security patches and software updates are essential to maintaining the integrity of RADIUS services. RADIUS server software, including open-source implementations like FreeRADIUS or commercial solutions, should be updated regularly to address known vulnerabilities and improve cryptographic support. In environments where compliance with regulatory standards such as PCI DSS, HIPAA, or ISO/IEC 27001 is required, maintaining up-to-date and secure RADIUS services is a mandatory component of broader network security controls.

When deploying RADIUS in federated authentication environments, such as eduroam or inter-organizational access agreements, additional care must be taken to ensure secure interconnection between RADIUS proxies and home servers. Federated networks often involve multiple administrative domains, each with its own security policies and practices. Ensuring that all participating organizations adhere to mutually agreed-upon security standards, including RadSec enforcement, certificate management, and access controls, is critical to protecting the integrity of the entire federation.

Finally, educating administrators and operators on best practices for securing RADIUS communications is an important part of maintaining a resilient and secure infrastructure. Regular training on secure configuration, incident response, and emerging threats helps ensure that security measures are correctly implemented and maintained over time. As the threat landscape continues to evolve, organizations must continuously assess and adapt their RADIUS security strategies to address new challenges and safeguard sensitive authentication data against compromise.

IPsec and TLS Encryption for RADIUS

IPsec and TLS encryption are two of the most widely adopted methods for securing RADIUS communications, providing essential protection for authentication, authorization, and accounting data as it traverses potentially insecure networks. While the RADIUS protocol was designed to perform basic security functions using shared secrets and MD5 hashing, these measures are no longer sufficient to defend against modern threats. Encrypting RADIUS traffic using IPsec or TLS mitigates the risks of eavesdropping, tampering, and replay attacks by introducing robust cryptographic protections at the transport or network layers.

IPsec operates at the network layer and is capable of securing all IP traffic between RADIUS clients and servers, not just RADIUS packets. This makes IPsec particularly appealing in environments where multiple services or protocols share the same communication channel and require comprehensive protection. IPsec can operate in two modes: transport mode and tunnel mode. Transport mode encrypts only the payload of each IP packet, leaving the header intact, which is typically used for host-to-host communication. Tunnel mode, on the other hand, encrypts the entire IP packet and encapsulates it within a new IP header, commonly used for gateway-to-gateway or site-to-site VPNs. When securing RADIUS traffic, both modes can be utilized depending on the network architecture and whether the encryption is being applied directly between NAS devices and RADIUS servers or across VPN concentrators.

Establishing an IPsec connection involves negotiating security associations (SAs) through protocols like Internet Key Exchange (IKE or IKEv2), which define the cryptographic algorithms, keys, and lifetimes used to secure the session. Encryption algorithms such as AES and authentication mechanisms like HMAC-SHA2 are typically selected to ensure strong confidentiality and integrity. Once established, the IPsec tunnel encrypts all data exchanged between endpoints, ensuring that sensitive authentication credentials and session attributes are shielded from interception or manipulation. IPsec also adds anti-replay protections by incorporating sequence numbers and integrity checks, preventing attackers from capturing and reusing legitimate RADIUS packets.

Despite its strengths, IPsec introduces operational complexity. It requires careful configuration of security policies, key management, and firewall rules to ensure seamless and secure communication between endpoints. Additionally, administrators must monitor and maintain IPsec tunnels to address potential issues such as tunnel drops, rekeying failures, or incompatibilities between different vendors' implementations. While these challenges are manageable with proper planning and automation, they are factors that organizations must consider when choosing IPsec as their primary RADIUS transport security mechanism.

TLS, specifically in the form of RADIUS over TLS (RadSec), is a transport layer solution that directly encrypts RADIUS packets, providing end-to-end confidentiality and integrity. RadSec encapsulates RADIUS traffic within a TLS session, similar to how HTTPS protects HTTP traffic. This approach is particularly well-suited for environments where RADIUS requests traverse untrusted networks, such as the public internet, or when implementing federated authentication frameworks. TLS encryption ensures that all RADIUS attributes, including usernames, service-type requests, and accounting information, are encrypted and protected from passive interception or active tampering.

RadSec requires the deployment of X.509 digital certificates for mutual authentication between RADIUS clients and servers. Both sides of the connection present certificates during the TLS handshake, and the certificates must be issued by a trusted Certificate Authority (CA) or belong to a trusted private PKI. The use of certificates not only secures the communication channel but also provides assurance of the identity of each party. Once the TLS session is established, standard RADIUS operations such as Access-Request, Access-Accept, and Accounting-Request proceed over the encrypted tunnel, preserving full protocol functionality while enhancing security.

Unlike IPsec, which operates transparently at the network level, RadSec is implemented directly within the RADIUS server software. Popular RADIUS servers like FreeRADIUS provide built-in support for RadSec, allowing administrators to configure TLS listeners and client-specific policies within the server's configuration files. TLS parameters, including cipher suites, key lengths, and protocol versions, can be adjusted to meet organizational security policies and compliance requirements. Strong cryptographic settings, such as enforcing TLS 1.2 or higher and using modern ciphers like AES-GCM, are recommended to ensure resilience against emerging threats.

One of the key advantages of RadSec over IPsec is its relative ease of deployment in multi-organization or federated environments. In scenarios such as eduroam or other roaming consortiums, RadSec is often the preferred method for securing inter-organizational RADIUS traffic due to its compatibility with existing PKI frameworks and its focus on application-layer security. By leveraging TLS, organizations can establish secure authentication channels across disparate administrative domains without the need for complex VPN tunnels or additional network-layer configurations.

Performance is another factor to consider when comparing IPsec and TLS encryption for RADIUS. Both protocols introduce encryption overhead, but TLS generally offers more fine-tuned control over session resumption and connection reuse through mechanisms like TLS session tickets or persistent connections. This can result in reduced latency and improved throughput in environments with high volumes of short-lived RADIUS transactions. IPsec, while highly secure, may introduce more significant latency in certain cases due to the additional encapsulation and processing requirements at the network layer.

From a security perspective, both IPsec and TLS are considered highly effective when implemented correctly. However, each method requires proper key and certificate management to prevent vulnerabilities. For IPsec, this includes securely managing pre-shared keys or digital certificates used during the IKE negotiation, as well as configuring appropriate lifetimes and rekeying intervals. For TLS, administrators must ensure that certificates are rotated before expiration, properly validate certificate chains, and implement revocation checks using methods such as CRLs or OCSP.

Organizations may also choose to deploy a hybrid approach, using both IPsec and RadSec depending on network segmentation, geographic distribution, and specific security policies. For instance, IPsec tunnels may be used to secure traffic between remote NAS devices and a central data center, while RadSec is employed to protect traffic between RADIUS proxies or between internal and external RADIUS servers participating in federated authentication.

Ultimately, the decision to implement IPsec or TLS encryption for RADIUS should be driven by a careful assessment of the network environment, regulatory requirements, performance needs, and operational complexity. Both solutions significantly enhance the security posture of the RADIUS infrastructure by safeguarding sensitive user credentials and accounting data. By deploying strong encryption mechanisms and maintaining rigorous key management practices, organizations can ensure that their RADIUS communications remain resilient against modern cyber threats and aligned with industry best practices.

Monitoring and Logging

Monitoring and logging are critical components in the management and security of any RADIUS deployment. These processes provide visibility into authentication, authorization, and accounting activities across the network, enabling administrators to detect anomalies, troubleshoot issues, and ensure compliance with security policies and regulatory standards. Without effective monitoring and logging, organizations are left blind to the operational state of their RADIUS servers, missing key insights into both routine network activity and potential security threats.

At the heart of RADIUS monitoring is the collection and analysis of detailed logs generated by the RADIUS server during its operation. Every authentication request, whether successful or failed, is logged along with relevant data such as timestamps, client IP addresses, usernames, NAS identifiers, and reasons for acceptance or rejection. These logs form the foundational layer of information for network administrators and security analysts. By reviewing these records, teams can identify patterns of usage, spot unauthorized access attempts, and correlate authentication events with user activity across the organization.

Logging is also essential for diagnosing configuration or performance issues within the RADIUS infrastructure. Misconfigured NAS clients, expired user credentials, or mismatched shared secrets between RADIUS servers and clients can all result in authentication failures.

Logs provide the forensic details necessary to pinpoint the root cause of such issues, reducing downtime and preventing disruptions to user access. Logs also play a role in fine-tuning authentication and accounting policies, helping administrators adjust session timeouts, refine access control rules, or optimize load balancing across multiple RADIUS servers.

To maximize the utility of RADIUS logs, organizations typically integrate them with centralized logging and monitoring systems. A common practice is to forward logs from multiple RADIUS servers to a centralized syslog server or Security Information and Event Management (SIEM) platform. This aggregation enables a unified view of authentication activity across distributed environments and enhances the ability to detect trends or correlated events that may not be apparent when reviewing isolated logs from individual servers. Centralized log management also streamlines incident response workflows, allowing security teams to quickly analyze data from multiple sources and coordinate appropriate actions when anomalies are detected.

The granularity and verbosity of RADIUS logs can be configured to suit the specific needs of the organization. While verbose logging provides a comprehensive view of every aspect of RADIUS transactions, including packet-level details and attribute values, it can generate large volumes of data, especially in high-traffic environments. Balancing the need for detailed insights with storage and processing constraints is key to designing an effective logging strategy. In some cases, organizations may configure their RADIUS servers to log all authentication attempts but selectively log accounting data or debug-level output only during troubleshooting sessions or audits.

Monitoring extends beyond basic log collection and includes real-time analysis of RADIUS server performance and health. Administrators must continuously track key performance indicators (KPIs) such as authentication request rates, response times, CPU and memory utilization, and disk I/O. Monitoring these metrics helps ensure that RADIUS servers are operating within expected parameters and alerts administrators to performance degradation or resource constraints before they impact network users. Automated monitoring tools can be configured to trigger alerts based on threshold violations, such as high failure rates, excessive latency, or resource exhaustion.

Availability monitoring is another crucial aspect of RADIUS server operations. Uptime monitoring tools verify that RADIUS services are responsive and accepting requests from NAS devices. Health checks may include simple tests such as verifying that the RADIUS process is running or more advanced probes that simulate authentication requests to ensure full functionality. Proactive availability monitoring reduces the risk of undetected outages or degraded service levels and supports high-availability and redundancy configurations by ensuring failover mechanisms are working as intended.

In security-focused environments, monitoring and logging also play a role in detecting and mitigating attacks against the RADIUS infrastructure. Brute-force attacks, where an attacker repeatedly submits authentication attempts in an effort to guess valid credentials, can be detected by analyzing logs for patterns such as multiple failed logins from a single IP address within a short period. Similarly, monitoring systems can flag signs of RADIUS-based denial-of-service (DoS) attacks, where the goal is to overwhelm the server with a high volume of authentication or accounting requests.

Integrating RADIUS logs into a SIEM platform enhances threat detection by applying correlation rules and behavioral analytics to authentication data. SIEM solutions can correlate RADIUS events with logs from other network devices, such as firewalls, intrusion detection systems, and endpoint protection tools, to create a more complete picture of security incidents. For example, a SIEM could detect a scenario where a compromised account is used to authenticate through RADIUS and then initiate unauthorized actions on a critical server. The ability to correlate and visualize such events is invaluable for incident responders.

Regulatory compliance is another reason monitoring and logging are non-negotiable in modern RADIUS environments. Regulations such as PCI DSS, HIPAA, GDPR, and ISO/IEC 27001 require organizations to maintain detailed logs of user authentication activity and retain these logs for specified periods. Logs must also be protected against tampering, requiring the implementation of secure log storage solutions and access controls. Failure to properly log and monitor RADIUS activities can result in non-compliance, exposing organizations to legal and financial penalties.

A growing trend in RADIUS monitoring is the adoption of cloud-native observability platforms that offer enhanced analytics, dashboards, and alerting capabilities. Tools like Prometheus and Grafana are increasingly used to visualize RADIUS server performance metrics, while cloud-based log analysis platforms such as Splunk, Elastic Stack, or SaaS SIEM offerings provide advanced search, filtering, and reporting functionalities. These solutions improve the accessibility and usability of monitoring data, helping administrators and security teams make data-driven decisions.

To further strengthen monitoring and logging, organizations should also consider integrating user behavior analytics (UBA) and machine learning-driven anomaly detection. These advanced techniques can analyze historical RADIUS log data to establish baselines of normal authentication behavior and then automatically detect deviations indicative of insider threats or compromised accounts. For instance, if a user suddenly authenticates from an unfamiliar geographic location or during unusual hours, automated monitoring tools can flag the event for review.

An effective RADIUS monitoring and logging strategy not only supports security and compliance but also improves operational efficiency. By maintaining comprehensive records of authentication activity and continuously assessing the health and performance of RADIUS servers, organizations can ensure the consistent delivery of authentication services, proactively resolve issues, and protect against evolving threats. Monitoring and logging remain foundational practices for any organization that depends on RADIUS to secure and manage access to its network infrastructure.

Auditing and Compliance

Auditing and compliance are critical aspects of managing RADIUS infrastructure in modern network environments. As organizations face increasing regulatory scrutiny and must demonstrate that they are following best practices to protect sensitive data and control user access, a robust auditing framework becomes essential. Auditing within a RADIUS context involves systematically collecting, reviewing, and analyzing authentication, authorization, and accounting records to ensure that all access events are properly logged, monitored, and evaluated against internal security policies and external regulatory standards.

At the core of RADIUS auditing is the requirement to maintain a complete and accurate record of user authentication attempts. Every successful and failed login event must be logged with key details such as the timestamp, the user's identity, the IP address of the NAS device, the result of the authentication attempt, and the reason for any rejection. These records provide the foundation for security audits, allowing organizations to demonstrate control over who is accessing network resources and under what conditions. Auditors will expect to see that the organization has mechanisms in place to track user activity and investigate anomalies or unauthorized access attempts effectively.

Compliance frameworks such as PCI DSS, HIPAA, ISO/IEC 27001, NIST 800-53, and GDPR include requirements related to identity and access management, making auditing of RADIUS services a fundamental control. For example, PCI DSS mandates that all access to cardholder data environments be monitored and that authentication logs are retained for at least one year, with the most recent three months readily available for review. In healthcare environments governed by HIPAA, organizations must ensure that all access to electronic protected health information (ePHI) is logged and auditable, which includes RADIUS-based access to wireless networks and VPNs used by healthcare staff.

Auditing is not limited to reviewing authentication events alone. Accounting data, which details how long a user session lasted, the amount of data transferred, and the termination cause, also plays an important role in auditing and compliance. Accounting logs allow organizations to monitor how network resources are being consumed and provide evidence that access is not only granted appropriately but also used responsibly. For organizations subject to regulatory reporting or billing requirements, such as ISPs or managed service providers, the accuracy of accounting data is critical for both financial and compliance purposes.

A comprehensive auditing strategy also requires a structured approach to log retention and protection. Auditors will review how long RADIUS logs are retained, where they are stored, and what measures are in place to ensure their integrity and confidentiality. Logs must be protected from unauthorized access or tampering, typically through file system permissions, encryption at rest, and secure transport mechanisms such as TLS or SSH when transmitting logs to centralized repositories. In environments where tamper-evidence is essential, organizations may implement log hashing or digital signing mechanisms to detect and prevent undetected modifications.

RADIUS auditing extends to configuration management as well. Auditors will assess how changes to RADIUS server configurations, including client definitions, authentication policies, and shared secrets, are tracked and controlled. Implementing version control systems and change management procedures helps demonstrate that all configuration changes are documented, reviewed, and authorized according to internal policies. Unauthorized or undocumented changes to RADIUS settings could introduce vulnerabilities or compliance violations, making change auditing an important aspect of the overall security program.

User access reviews are another key component of RADIUS auditing and compliance efforts. Organizations must periodically review which users have access to critical network systems and ensure that their access rights align with their current roles and responsibilities. In the context of RADIUS, this might include reviewing which users or groups are authorized to authenticate to specific NAS devices or network segments and whether those permissions remain appropriate. Auditors will often request evidence of these access reviews and expect organizations to demonstrate that inactive or unnecessary accounts are promptly disabled or removed.

Auditing also plays a role in incident response and forensic investigations. In the event of a security breach or suspected policy violation, RADIUS logs provide critical data points that help investigators understand the timeline of events, identify compromised accounts, and determine the scope of unauthorized access. A well-maintained audit trail enables organizations to respond to incidents more effectively, limit potential damage, and comply with breach notification requirements that may apply under specific regulations such as GDPR.

In federated authentication environments, where RADIUS traffic may traverse multiple administrative domains, auditing requirements can become even more complex. Organizations participating in federations like eduroam must ensure that their RADIUS infrastructure complies with both local regulatory obligations and federation-wide policies. This may include ensuring that RADIUS proxies log and forward requests in a compliant manner and that cross-domain authentication events are auditable by both the originating and destination organizations.

Compliance efforts often culminate in formal audits conducted by internal teams or external assessors. During these audits, organizations must present documentation detailing their RADIUS logging practices, log review procedures, incident response plans, and evidence of past log reviews or access control assessments. Auditors may also interview staff responsible for RADIUS operations to verify that logging and auditing processes are consistently followed and that personnel understand their roles in maintaining compliance.

Automation can greatly enhance RADIUS auditing and compliance capabilities. Integrating RADIUS logs with SIEM platforms allows for real-time monitoring and automated alerting on suspicious activities, such as repeated failed login attempts, authentication requests from unexpected geographic regions, or signs of brute-force attacks. SIEM tools can also generate regular compliance reports that summarize key metrics, including the number of authentication events, failures, and anomalies detected over a specified period, providing valuable insights for both auditors and security teams.

Training and awareness are important elements of any auditing and compliance program. Personnel responsible for managing RADIUS servers and monitoring logs should receive regular training on regulatory requirements, emerging threats, and best practices for maintaining secure and auditable environments. Ensuring that teams are aware of their responsibilities and capable of detecting and responding to potential compliance issues is crucial to the ongoing success of the auditing program.

Ultimately, auditing and compliance in the context of RADIUS are about demonstrating accountability and control over network access management. By maintaining comprehensive audit trails, securing log data, and aligning operational practices with relevant regulations and industry standards, organizations can protect sensitive data, reduce the risk of security breaches, and confidently demonstrate compliance to stakeholders, customers, and regulatory bodies.

Troubleshooting RADIUS Authentication Issues

Troubleshooting RADIUS authentication issues is a critical skill for network and system administrators, as RADIUS is often a central component of network security and access control mechanisms. When RADIUS authentication fails, users may experience denied access to wireless networks, VPNs, or other resources, leading to productivity disruptions and security concerns. The troubleshooting process requires a systematic approach, beginning with understanding the flow of RADIUS communication and narrowing down where within that flow the problem may exist. Since RADIUS authentication involves multiple components, including the client (NAS device), the RADIUS server, and potentially a backend identity store such as LDAP or Active Directory, any one of these elements could be the source of the issue.

The first step in troubleshooting RADIUS authentication problems is to verify the NAS configuration. A misconfigured NAS is a common culprit in RADIUS failures. The NAS must have the correct IP address and shared secret configured to match the details stored on the RADIUS server. A mismatch in the shared secret, for instance, will cause the RADIUS server to reject requests or fail to recognize them altogether. Additionally, administrators should confirm that the NAS is pointing to the correct RADIUS server IP address and port, typically UDP port 1812 for authentication requests and 1813 for accounting.

Network connectivity between the NAS and the RADIUS server should be verified as well, ensuring that firewalls are not blocking the relevant ports and that routing is functioning as expected.

Once NAS configurations have been verified, attention should turn to the RADIUS server itself. Reviewing the RADIUS server logs is often the most informative step in identifying why authentication is failing. Logs may reveal common errors such as invalid user credentials, unsupported authentication methods, expired accounts, or misconfigured client definitions. A frequent issue is that the RADIUS server is not recognizing the NAS as a valid client because its IP address has not been properly configured or authorized within the server's client configuration files. In some cases, issues may stem from incorrect or missing attribute values in the Access-Request packet sent by the NAS.

Another common point of failure involves the authentication protocol being used. Many RADIUS servers and NAS devices support multiple authentication methods, including PAP, CHAP, MS-CHAPv2, EAP-TLS, and PEAP. Incompatibilities between the NAS and the RADIUS server regarding supported protocols can result in authentication failures. For example, if the NAS is configured to use MS-CHAPv2 but the RADIUS server does not support or has not been properly configured for that protocol, the authentication request will fail. Reviewing both the NAS and RADIUS configurations for protocol alignment is essential. Similarly, EAP-based protocols often require additional considerations, such as certificate validation when using EAP-TLS or PEAP, and improper certificate installation or trust issues can cause authentication to break down.

In environments where RADIUS integrates with an external identity store, such as Active Directory or an LDAP directory, it is necessary to validate the connection and binding credentials used by the RADIUS server to communicate with the backend. Incorrect bind DN, expired service account credentials, or network issues preventing communication with the directory server can all result in user authentication failures. Logs will often indicate specific errors, such as failed LDAP bind attempts or inability to locate user entries. Additionally, administrators should verify that the RADIUS server has appropriate read permissions on the directory to retrieve necessary user attributes.

Timeouts are another frequent issue encountered during RADIUS troubleshooting. If the NAS does not receive a timely response from the RADIUS server, it may assume the server is offline or unreachable, causing authentication to fail. Timeouts can result from high latency, overloaded servers, or improperly tuned timeout settings on the NAS or RADIUS server. Adjusting timeout and retry settings can help accommodate variations in network conditions or server response times.

It is also important to consider the possibility of accounting-related failures. Although accounting is separate from authentication, some NAS devices require successful accounting start messages to fully complete the session initiation. If the accounting port (usually UDP 1813) is blocked, misconfigured, or the RADIUS server fails to process accounting packets correctly, session establishment may be impacted.

RADIUS proxies introduce additional complexity when troubleshooting authentication issues. In federated or multi-tenant environments where RADIUS requests are forwarded through one or more proxies, failures can occur at any point along the forwarding chain. Administrators must verify that routing rules, shared secrets, and transport security (such as RadSec or IPsec) are correctly configured across all involved servers. Each proxy along the chain should be monitored to ensure that requests are being forwarded appropriately and that response packets are returning to the originating NAS device without alteration or loss.

Certificate issues are a leading cause of authentication failures when using EAP methods like EAP-TLS or PEAP. Certificates must be valid, signed by a trusted Certificate Authority, and installed correctly on both the RADIUS server and client devices. Expired certificates, mismatched certificate chains, or failure to trust the CA on client devices will cause EAP sessions to terminate during the TLS handshake. Detailed debugging logs from the RADIUS server can reveal handshake failures and point to certificate validation errors.

To ensure a comprehensive troubleshooting process, packet captures using tools like Wireshark can be invaluable. By capturing RADIUS traffic between the NAS and the server, administrators can inspect packet contents, verify attribute values, and observe protocol-level exchanges. Wireshark dissectors for RADIUS provide clear views into Access-Request, Access-Challenge, Access-Accept, and Access-Reject messages, as well as EAP payloads in tunneled authentication scenarios. This level of analysis is particularly useful for diagnosing subtle issues, such as incorrect formatting of RADIUS attributes or missing mandatory fields.

A methodical approach to troubleshooting RADIUS authentication also includes reviewing network performance and system health. High CPU or memory usage on the RADIUS server may cause delays in processing requests, while network congestion or dropped packets could lead to sporadic authentication failures. Regular monitoring of server and network performance metrics helps administrators identify resource bottlenecks contributing to authentication issues.

Finally, documentation and knowledge sharing are key to successful long-term management of RADIUS environments. Maintaining detailed records of common troubleshooting steps, previous incidents, and their resolutions enables teams to respond more quickly to recurring issues. By applying a structured, step-by-step methodology to troubleshooting RADIUS authentication problems, organizations can minimize downtime, ensure reliable access to critical network resources, and maintain a secure and efficient authentication infrastructure.

Performance Tuning and Optimization

Performance tuning and optimization of RADIUS servers are essential to ensure the smooth operation of authentication, authorization, and accounting services, particularly in large-scale or high-demand environments. As RADIUS plays a crucial role in controlling user access across VPNs, wireless networks, wired infrastructures, and other network services, any latency or performance bottleneck can lead to slow logins, user dissatisfaction, and potential security risks. Achieving optimal RADIUS server performance involves analyzing and improving various layers of the system, including server hardware, network configurations, database interactions, and the RADIUS server software itself.

A fundamental step in performance tuning is ensuring that the hardware running the RADIUS server is appropriately sized for the workload it must handle. RADIUS servers process hundreds or even thousands of authentication requests per second in large enterprises or service provider networks. To support such demand, the underlying server should be equipped with sufficient CPU cores, memory, and disk I/O capacity. Multi-core processors enable parallel processing of RADIUS requests, reducing response times and preventing CPU bottlenecks. Ample memory is necessary to cache frequently accessed data, such as user profiles, policies, or TLS session information, thereby reducing the load on external databases or backend identity stores.

Network optimization is equally critical for RADIUS performance. RADIUS typically operates over UDP, which is a connectionless protocol and sensitive to packet loss and latency. To minimize these risks, administrators must ensure that the network infrastructure connecting NAS devices to the RADIUS servers is reliable and has low-latency, high-bandwidth connections. Network devices such as firewalls, routers, and switches should be configured to prioritize RADIUS traffic, avoiding unnecessary delays caused by congestion or QoS misconfigurations. It is also important to monitor for dropped or fragmented packets that could interfere with RADIUS communication, especially in networks with VPN tunnels or security appliances performing deep packet inspection.

Another key factor in optimizing RADIUS performance is fine-tuning the server's configuration settings. RADIUS servers, such as FreeRADIUS, include various tunable parameters that directly impact their responsiveness. For instance, administrators can adjust the number of worker threads or server processes that handle incoming requests. Increasing the number of threads can improve throughput, allowing the server to process more concurrent authentication or accounting requests. However, this must be balanced against available system resources to avoid overcommitting CPU or memory capacity.

Timeouts and retransmission settings should also be reviewed and adjusted according to the network's characteristics. RADIUS servers and NAS clients typically have configurable timeout values that dictate how long they wait for a response before resending a request or failing the authentication attempt. Optimizing these values is crucial in minimizing unnecessary retransmissions that can contribute to server load and network congestion. In well-performing networks, shorter timeout values may be appropriate, while higher-latency environments may require slightly longer timeouts to accommodate packet travel times.

For RADIUS servers integrated with external identity stores, such as LDAP directories or SQL databases, the performance of these backends significantly affects overall authentication speed. Optimizing LDAP queries by limiting the scope of searches, indexing frequently queried attributes, and maintaining a healthy directory structure reduces lookup times and accelerates user authentication. Similarly, when using SQL databases to store user credentials or accounting data, administrators should ensure that queries are well-optimized and that proper indexing is applied to relevant database fields. Database connection pooling can also enhance performance by reducing the overhead of repeatedly opening and closing connections during peak usage periods.

TLS encryption, often used in EAP methods such as EAP-TLS or PEAP, introduces additional computational overhead due to the encryption and decryption of traffic. While necessary for securing authentication sessions, TLS-related processing can be resource-intensive, particularly in environments with large numbers of concurrent connections. Optimizing TLS settings, such as enabling session resumption with session tickets or session IDs, can significantly reduce the load on the RADIUS server by avoiding full handshake renegotiations for each session. Choosing efficient cryptographic ciphers, such as AES-GCM, can further reduce CPU consumption without compromising security.

Load balancing is another essential optimization strategy for environments where a single RADIUS server cannot meet the demand alone. By distributing incoming requests across multiple RADIUS servers using round-robin, least-connections, or weighted load-balancing algorithms, organizations can ensure that no single server becomes a bottleneck. This not only enhances performance but also provides redundancy and fault tolerance. Load balancing can be performed at the network level using dedicated appliances or software-based solutions like HAProxy, or by configuring NAS devices to failover between multiple RADIUS servers.

Caching mechanisms play a significant role in accelerating repeated requests and reducing backend dependencies. Some RADIUS servers allow caching of authorization policies, user group memberships, or other session-related attributes. By storing frequently accessed information locally for a defined period, the server can avoid repetitive queries to backend systems, improving response times during periods of high activity.

Monitoring and performance metrics collection are vital to effective optimization. Administrators should regularly monitor authentication response times, server CPU and memory usage, disk I/O, and network statistics. By establishing baselines and identifying trends or spikes, teams can proactively address performance degradation before it impacts users. Logs and metrics should be collected and analyzed to identify bottlenecks, such as consistently slow queries to a directory server or high CPU usage during TLS handshakes.

Security-related features, such as logging verbosity, can also affect RADIUS performance. While verbose logging is useful during troubleshooting, it may introduce overhead during normal operations, especially on busy servers. Administrators should strike a balance by retaining essential logging while disabling excessive debug-level outputs during routine operation. Logs should be forwarded to centralized servers to reduce the load on local storage and avoid disk space exhaustion.

As RADIUS is often part of larger, distributed network architectures, administrators must also consider the performance impact of external factors, such as the performance of upstream proxies, federation components, or cross-site latency. In federated environments, where RADIUS requests may traverse multiple proxies before reaching the home server, each additional hop introduces potential delays. Optimizing proxy routing rules, ensuring efficient TLS session establishment, and minimizing the number of forwarding layers can collectively enhance end-to-end performance.

Ultimately, performance tuning and optimization of RADIUS environments require a holistic approach that considers every component involved in the authentication process. From hardware and network infrastructure to software configuration and backend integrations, each layer must be carefully reviewed and adjusted to achieve the best possible performance. A well-tuned RADIUS deployment not only ensures fast and reliable user access but also strengthens security and contributes to the overall efficiency of the organization's IT infrastructure.

Scalability Strategies

Scalability strategies for RADIUS infrastructures are essential to ensure that authentication, authorization, and accounting services can accommodate growth in users, devices, and network complexity. As organizations expand their operations or as service providers onboard new customers, the RADIUS system must be capable of handling increasing authentication loads without introducing latency, bottlenecks, or single points of failure. Effective scalability planning focuses on designing an architecture that grows horizontally or vertically, depending on demand, while maintaining service reliability, performance, and security.

One of the most fundamental scalability strategies is horizontal scaling, which involves deploying multiple RADIUS servers to distribute the load across several nodes. This approach allows organizations to add new servers as demand increases, preventing any single server from becoming overwhelmed. In a horizontally scaled deployment, RADIUS servers operate in parallel and share the workload, providing redundancy and load balancing. By leveraging network-level load balancers or configuring Network Access Servers (NAS) to distribute authentication requests across multiple RADIUS servers, organizations can ensure even resource utilization and improve the system's ability to handle spikes in authentication activity.

Vertical scaling, on the other hand, focuses on increasing the capabilities of individual RADIUS servers by upgrading hardware resources, such as adding more CPU cores, memory, or faster storage. While vertical scaling can enhance performance in the short term, it has practical limitations, as there is a finite capacity to which a single server can be expanded. Therefore, vertical scaling is often combined with horizontal strategies to achieve long-term scalability. In high-demand environments, it is common to first optimize individual server performance and then deploy additional servers as necessary.

Database scalability is equally critical in RADIUS environments where external databases, such as SQL or LDAP directories, are used to store user credentials, policies, or accounting data. As authentication requests grow, the backend database can become a bottleneck if it is not scaled appropriately. Implementing database replication or clustering can help distribute query loads and enhance fault tolerance. For example, read-intensive queries, such as user lookups during authentication, can be directed to database replicas, reducing the load on the primary server. Write-heavy workloads, such as accounting logs, may require specialized architectures like database sharding to distribute data across multiple servers efficiently.

Caching mechanisms are another effective scalability strategy. By caching frequently accessed data, such as user group memberships or authentication policies, RADIUS servers can reduce the frequency and load of database queries. Caching reduces latency and alleviates backend pressure during peak traffic periods. Some RADIUS implementations, like FreeRADIUS, support built-in caching modules, while others can be integrated with external caching systems such as Memcached or Redis. Proper cache management, including setting appropriate cache lifetimes and invalidation policies, is important to ensure that cached data remains current and accurate.

Geographical distribution of RADIUS servers is critical for organizations with a global footprint or for service providers operating across multiple regions. Deploying RADIUS servers in multiple data centers or points of presence (PoPs) close to the users and NAS devices reduces latency and improves user experience. Geographic redundancy also enhances resiliency by ensuring that a failure in one region does not affect users in other locations. In distributed architectures, Global

Server Load Balancing (GSLB) techniques can be used to direct authentication requests to the nearest available RADIUS server based on client location or network conditions.

Automation and orchestration tools are becoming increasingly important in scalable RADIUS environments. Tools like Ansible, Terraform, or Kubernetes enable administrators to rapidly deploy, configure, and scale RADIUS servers across cloud or on-premises environments. Automated deployments reduce human error, speed up provisioning times, and ensure consistency across multiple servers. For containerized RADIUS deployments, orchestration platforms like Kubernetes offer additional scalability benefits, such as auto-scaling based on CPU or memory usage, self-healing, and rolling updates without service downtime.

Load balancing plays a key role in distributing traffic across scalable RADIUS infrastructures. Whether using hardware load balancers, software-based solutions like HAProxy, or DNS-based techniques such as round-robin, the objective is to ensure that no single RADIUS server bears a disproportionate share of the load. Load balancers also improve fault tolerance by rerouting traffic away from failed or degraded servers to maintain service continuity. More advanced load-balancing techniques may include weighted algorithms that take into account each server's performance capacity or real-time health checks to route requests intelligently.

Scalability strategies must also address the security implications of expansion. As more servers are deployed across a growing network, ensuring that all RADIUS nodes adhere to consistent security configurations is essential. Automated configuration management tools help enforce uniform settings for shared secrets, TLS certificates, authentication policies, and logging practices across all RADIUS servers. Maintaining consistency helps reduce vulnerabilities that could arise from misconfigured servers or outdated security practices.

Monitoring and analytics are vital for supporting scalable RADIUS deployments. As the infrastructure grows, the ability to collect and analyze metrics from all servers becomes crucial for capacity planning and proactive performance tuning. Metrics such as authentication request rates, CPU and memory utilization, database query performance, and network latency provide insight into when additional scaling actions may be necessary. Centralized monitoring platforms, such as Prometheus with Grafana dashboards, allow administrators to visualize trends and set alerts when thresholds are exceeded.

In cloud-based or hybrid environments, elasticity becomes an important scalability factor. Cloud-native RADIUS implementations can take advantage of infrastructure-as-a-service (IaaS) offerings from providers like AWS, Azure, or Google Cloud to dynamically scale instances based on real-time demand. For example, auto-scaling groups in AWS can automatically launch or terminate RADIUS server instances depending on CPU usage or incoming request volume. This flexibility ensures that resources are used efficiently and that the infrastructure can adapt to fluctuating workloads without manual intervention.

Federated authentication scenarios, such as eduroam or other roaming services, also benefit from scalable RADIUS designs. In these environments, where authentication requests may be forwarded across multiple proxies and organizations, scalable proxy servers and redundant paths ensure that increased traffic volumes do not degrade authentication performance. Each organization participating in a federation must ensure that its RADIUS infrastructure can handle peak loads while maintaining low latency across federated boundaries.

Scalability is not only about handling more traffic but also about maintaining operational efficiency as the infrastructure grows. Documentation, standard operating procedures, and well-defined workflows for scaling up or down help teams manage larger RADIUS deployments with reduced complexity. Investing in training for operational staff and ensuring cross-team coordination between network, security, and system administrators further supports smooth scalability transitions.

Ultimately, a successful RADIUS scalability strategy is multifaceted, combining horizontal and vertical scaling, distributed deployments, automation, load balancing, and strong backend database design. By addressing each of these layers thoughtfully, organizations can build RADIUS infrastructures capable of supporting expanding user bases, increased authentication loads, and the evolving needs of modern networks. Scalability planning should be ongoing, with continuous assessment and adjustment to meet changing business requirements and technology landscapes.

Deploying RADIUS in Enterprise Networks

Deploying RADIUS in enterprise networks is a fundamental step in establishing a secure, scalable, and centralized access control system. As enterprises increasingly adopt hybrid environments that integrate wireless and wired networks, virtual private networks (VPNs), and cloud-based applications, the need for a unified authentication, authorization, and accounting (AAA) solution becomes critical. RADIUS provides enterprises with a standardized protocol to manage user and device access, enforce security policies, and maintain detailed activity records across various network segments and access technologies.

The deployment process begins with a clear understanding of the network topology and the identification of systems and devices that will rely on the RADIUS infrastructure. Common RADIUS clients in enterprise networks include wireless LAN controllers, switches implementing 802.1X for port-based access control, VPN concentrators, firewalls, and other NAS devices. Each of these clients will communicate with one or more RADIUS servers to request authentication and authorization decisions for users attempting to connect to the network. To ensure high availability and redundancy, enterprises typically deploy multiple RADIUS servers in an active-active or active-passive configuration, distributing the load and providing failover capabilities.

One of the critical considerations during deployment is the integration of RADIUS with existing identity management systems. In most enterprises, user credentials and group memberships are stored in centralized directories such as Microsoft Active Directory (AD) or LDAP-compliant services. The RADIUS server must be configured to authenticate users against these directories, often leveraging protocols like LDAP or Kerberos. This integration ensures that authentication policies are consistent with the organization's security framework and that user management remains centralized and efficient. When integrated with AD, RADIUS can enforce granular access control policies based on group memberships, organizational units, or specific user attributes.

Authentication methods play a vital role in determining the security and compatibility of the deployment. Enterprises deploying RADIUS typically select Extensible Authentication Protocol (EAP) methods appropriate to their security requirements and the capabilities of client devices. EAP-TLS, which relies on mutual certificate-based authentication, is widely regarded as one of the most secure methods and is favored in environments where a public key infrastructure (PKI) is available. PEAP-MSCHAPv2, another popular choice, encapsulates user credentials within a secure TLS tunnel and is often deployed where password-based authentication is required but encryption is also necessary. The choice of EAP method influences both the security posture of the network and the end-user experience.

Once the RADIUS server is configured and integrated with the enterprise's directory services, attention shifts to configuring RADIUS clients. Each NAS device must be provided with the IP address of the RADIUS server(s) and the shared secret used to secure RADIUS communications. Enterprises must ensure that shared secrets are strong, unique per client, and securely stored to prevent unauthorized access. In addition to basic connectivity, NAS devices often require configuration of the authentication method (e.g., 802.1X or MAC authentication), VLAN assignments based on RADIUS responses, and fallback options in case of RADIUS server unavailability.

The RADIUS deployment must also address accounting and logging requirements. Enterprises use RADIUS accounting to record session start and stop times, the amount of data transferred, and other session attributes. These logs serve multiple purposes, including compliance reporting, troubleshooting, and capacity planning. Integrating RADIUS accounting logs with a centralized logging system or Security Information and Event Management (SIEM) platform enhances visibility across the enterprise network and supports incident response efforts.

Security hardening of the RADIUS infrastructure is a non-negotiable element of enterprise deployments. Administrators must restrict RADIUS communication to trusted networks and devices by configuring firewalls and access control lists (ACLs). Where possible, RADIUS traffic should be encrypted using RADIUS over TLS (RadSec) or IPsec tunnels, particularly in networks where authentication requests traverse untrusted or public segments. Enabling secure protocols helps protect sensitive data, such as usernames and passwords, from interception and tampering.

To support enterprise-scale deployments, RADIUS servers should be optimized for performance and scalability. This involves tuning server parameters to handle expected authentication loads, configuring multiple worker threads, and ensuring adequate hardware resources. Enterprises may also implement load balancing, using solutions such as HAProxy or commercial load balancers, to evenly distribute RADIUS requests across multiple servers. Geographically distributed enterprises often deploy RADIUS servers in regional data centers, improving performance for remote sites and providing regional redundancy.

The deployment process is not complete without robust monitoring and alerting mechanisms. Enterprises must monitor RADIUS server health, authentication response times, and system resource utilization to identify potential issues before they impact users. Centralized monitoring platforms, such as Prometheus combined with Grafana dashboards, offer valuable insights into RADIUS server metrics and can trigger automated alerts in the event of anomalies, such as high failure rates or server outages.

Policy enforcement is another layer of enterprise RADIUS deployments. RADIUS supports dynamic authorization, allowing the server to send customized attribute-value pairs (AVPs) in Access-Accept responses. These attributes may dictate VLAN assignment, bandwidth limits, session timeout values, or access restrictions based on user roles or device characteristics. For example, employees might be placed in secure VLANs with full access, while guest users are assigned to isolated VLANs with restricted internet-only access. Enterprises can also leverage role-based access control (RBAC) frameworks within RADIUS to align network access with business requirements and security policies.

Enterprises must also plan for user experience when deploying RADIUS. User onboarding processes, such as distributing client certificates for EAP-TLS or configuring supplicant settings for 802.1X authentication, should be streamlined to minimize disruptions. Self-service portals, onboarding tools, or integration with mobile device management (MDM) platforms can simplify the configuration process for end users while enforcing compliance with security policies. In wireless environments, configuring Wi-Fi profiles that automate 802.1X authentication enhances usability and reduces support tickets related to authentication failures.

Documentation and training are critical to the long-term success of a RADIUS deployment. Network and security teams must maintain up-to-date documentation detailing server configurations, network diagrams, authentication policies, and operational procedures. Regular training sessions ensure that administrators remain proficient in managing and troubleshooting the RADIUS infrastructure as the enterprise grows and evolves.

Deploying RADIUS in enterprise networks lays the foundation for secure and centralized access control. By designing an infrastructure that is scalable, resilient, and aligned with organizational security objectives, enterprises can confidently protect their network resources while delivering a seamless authentication experience to users across a diverse array of devices and network access points. As technology evolves and new security challenges emerge, enterprises must continuously evaluate and refine their RADIUS deployments to ensure they meet modern requirements and best practices.

Using RADIUS in ISP Environments

Using RADIUS in ISP environments is a fundamental requirement for managing the authentication, authorization, and accounting of thousands, and often millions, of subscribers. Internet Service Providers rely heavily on RADIUS to validate user credentials, enforce access policies, and collect detailed accounting records for billing and operational analytics. The distributed nature of ISP networks, combined with the need for high availability and massive scalability, makes RADIUS an ideal choice for handling AAA functions in these large-scale environments.

At the core of an ISP's RADIUS deployment is the need to authenticate a wide variety of user connections, including broadband subscribers, wireless customers, enterprise clients using leased-line services, and VPN users. Each of these access types generates authentication requests that must be processed quickly and reliably. For broadband access, RADIUS often works in conjunction with PPPoE (Point-to-Point Protocol over Ethernet) or DHCP systems, validating customer credentials when they initiate a connection through modems, customer premises equipment (CPE), or other last-mile technologies such as DSL, fiber, or cable.

RADIUS provides the flexibility to integrate with backend subscriber databases, which in ISP environments are typically housed in SQL databases or LDAP directories. These databases contain customer account information, including usernames, passwords, service profiles, and status indicators. When a subscriber attempts to connect, the Network Access Server (NAS) or Broadband Remote Access Server (BRAS) forwards the authentication request to the RADIUS server, which queries the backend system to verify the subscriber's identity. This process ensures that only valid, active accounts are permitted to access ISP resources.

One of the key challenges in ISP environments is managing diverse subscriber service profiles. ISPs often offer multiple tiers of service, such as basic internet access, premium plans with higher bandwidth, or additional services like IPTV or VoIP. RADIUS facilitates this by returning specific attribute-value pairs (AVPs) during the authorization phase. For instance, the RADIUS server may include attributes that define bandwidth limits, Quality of Service (QoS) parameters, VLAN assignments, or dynamic IP address allocation. This enables ISPs to enforce differentiated services directly through the RADIUS infrastructure without requiring manual intervention or complex configurations on edge devices.

Accounting is another critical function provided by RADIUS in ISP environments. Accurate accounting records are essential for generating customer invoices, monitoring network usage, and complying with regulatory requirements. RADIUS accounting messages capture session start and stop times, the total volume of data transmitted and received, the duration of the session, and any additional session-specific information. These records are typically fed into mediation platforms or billing systems that process the raw data and generate invoices for subscribers based on their service plans and consumption patterns.

Scalability is an inherent requirement for RADIUS deployments in ISPs. A single RADIUS server cannot typically handle the sheer volume of authentication and accounting requests generated by thousands or millions of subscribers. To address this, ISPs deploy multiple RADIUS servers distributed across various geographic locations, often aligned with regional points of presence (PoPs) or data centers. Load balancing is applied at the NAS level or through dedicated load balancers to ensure even distribution of requests and to provide redundancy. In addition, RADIUS proxies are often used to route requests to the appropriate backend servers based on subscriber location, service type, or customer segment.

Security is paramount in ISP RADIUS deployments, as the infrastructure processes highly sensitive data, including subscriber credentials and billing information. ISP networks are frequently targeted by attackers seeking to disrupt service or gain unauthorized access to customer accounts. To mitigate these risks, ISPs implement security measures such as strong shared secrets between NAS devices and RADIUS servers, IP whitelisting to limit which devices can communicate with the RADIUS infrastructure, and encrypted communications using IPsec or RadSec (RADIUS over TLS) to protect traffic from eavesdropping and tampering.

The complexity of ISP networks often leads to the need for hierarchical RADIUS architectures. In such setups, regional or access-level RADIUS servers may forward requests to centralized or national-level servers, where business logic, policy enforcement, and billing integration are centralized. This layered approach ensures efficient handling of authentication requests while allowing local servers to offload basic tasks and caching functions, reducing response times for routine authentication and authorization decisions.

In addition to supporting traditional broadband and wired customers, RADIUS is extensively used by ISPs that provide wireless services. For Wi-Fi networks, including municipal hotspots or enterprise Wi-Fi solutions offered as managed services, RADIUS facilitates 802.1X authentication, allowing ISPs to authenticate users against their subscriber database. Wireless access controllers act as NAS clients, forwarding authentication and accounting messages to the ISP's RADIUS infrastructure. The use of RADIUS in wireless deployments enables ISPs to apply subscriber-specific policies, such as bandwidth limits or roaming restrictions, at the time of authentication.

RADIUS also plays a crucial role in supporting roaming agreements and partnerships between ISPs. When subscribers access networks operated by partner ISPs, RADIUS proxies forward authentication requests to the home ISP's RADIUS servers, enabling seamless cross-network authentication and service delivery. This is commonly seen in Wi-Fi roaming federations or wholesale broadband agreements where subscribers use multiple networks but are authenticated against a central subscriber database.

Monitoring and analytics are essential for maintaining the health and performance of RADIUS systems in ISP environments. ISPs deploy comprehensive monitoring solutions that track server health, authentication response times, accounting success rates, and overall system load. These metrics are critical for capacity planning, ensuring that the infrastructure can accommodate growth in subscriber numbers and usage patterns. Proactive monitoring also helps detect anomalies, such as spikes in failed authentication attempts, which may indicate security incidents or customer service issues.

Automation is increasingly integrated into RADIUS workflows to improve operational efficiency for ISPs. By automating provisioning processes, such as the creation or suspension of subscriber accounts, ISPs reduce the risk of manual errors and accelerate service activation times. APIs and orchestration tools can interface with the RADIUS infrastructure to dynamically update service profiles, enforce usage caps, or apply temporary access restrictions based on customer status or billing events.

The successful deployment of RADIUS in ISP environments requires ongoing collaboration between network, security, and operations teams. Careful planning, including capacity analysis, redundancy design, and policy standardization, ensures that the RADIUS infrastructure remains reliable and scalable as customer demands evolve. RADIUS continues to be a foundational technology for ISPs, providing a flexible and efficient mechanism to manage network access while enabling differentiated services, accurate billing, and strong security controls across a diverse and dynamic customer base.

RADIUS and Cloud Authentication

RADIUS and cloud authentication are increasingly intertwined as organizations migrate critical IT services and infrastructure to cloud environments. Traditionally, RADIUS has been deployed on-premises to provide authentication, authorization, and accounting for users and devices accessing local area networks, wireless networks, VPNs, and other on-premises systems. However, as enterprises embrace cloud-first strategies and hybrid infrastructures, RADIUS has evolved to integrate with cloud-based identity providers and services, enabling secure access control across both on-premises and cloud-hosted resources.

The foundation of using RADIUS with cloud authentication lies in extending RADIUS capabilities beyond the traditional network perimeter. In modern architectures, employees, partners, and contractors frequently access systems from remote locations or via cloud-hosted applications and platforms. This shift has necessitated the adoption of federated authentication models where cloud identity providers such as Azure Active Directory, Okta, Google Workspace, or AWS IAM serve as centralized identity sources. By integrating RADIUS with these identity platforms, organizations can centralize user management while retaining the ability to authenticate users on legacy systems, VPNs, or 802.1X-enabled networks.

One common deployment model involves using RADIUS servers as intermediaries between network access infrastructure, such as wireless controllers or VPN gateways, and the cloud identity provider. When a user initiates a connection to a VPN or Wi-Fi network, the NAS device sends the authentication request to the on-premises or cloud-hosted RADIUS server. The RADIUS server then performs an identity lookup against the cloud identity provider via protocols like SAML, OAuth2, or OpenID Connect. This federation of identity allows cloud-based user credentials to be seamlessly leveraged for network access without duplicating user directories across multiple systems.

Cloud-hosted RADIUS services are also gaining popularity. Several vendors now offer RADIUS-as-a-Service, where the RADIUS infrastructure is entirely hosted and managed in the cloud. These solutions reduce the burden of maintaining physical or virtual servers, managing patches, and ensuring high availability. Cloud RADIUS services typically provide API integrations with popular identity providers, allowing organizations to enforce multifactor authentication (MFA) policies, user risk scoring, or conditional access rules at the point of authentication. Cloud-based RADIUS platforms are particularly well-suited for organizations that have already shifted directory services to the cloud and are looking to offload the operational complexity associated with maintaining a RADIUS infrastructure.

For organizations with hybrid environments, combining on-premises RADIUS servers with cloud authentication enables secure access to both local and cloud-hosted applications. For instance, a company may operate RADIUS servers in regional offices to support wired and wireless network access while federating authentication to Azure AD for identity verification. This hybrid model provides the flexibility to authenticate users regardless of their physical location and ensures consistent security policies across different environments. It also allows enterprises to leverage cloud-based identity governance features such as automated deprovisioning, passwordless authentication methods, and centralized access reviews.

The use of cloud-based MFA is a key benefit when integrating RADIUS with cloud authentication platforms. Traditional RADIUS deployments often rely on single-factor authentication methods like passwords, but when combined with a cloud identity provider, RADIUS workflows can enforce MFA for all network access attempts. For example, when a user connects to the enterprise VPN, the RADIUS server may validate their username and password against the cloud provider and trigger a second authentication factor, such as a push notification to a mobile authenticator app or a biometric verification. This layered security approach significantly reduces the risk of credential-based attacks, which are common in remote access scenarios.

RADIUS and cloud authentication are also heavily used to support bring-your-own-device (BYOD) and guest access policies. In environments where employees use personal devices or guests require network access, cloud-integrated RADIUS servers can dynamically assign VLANs or apply access policies based on user roles defined in the cloud directory. For instance, employee devices may be placed on internal VLANs with access to corporate resources, while guest users are routed to isolated VLANs with restricted internet-only access. By leveraging group memberships or custom attributes within the cloud identity provider, the RADIUS server can make real-time authorization decisions aligned with organizational policies.

Security is a primary concern when integrating RADIUS with cloud services. Encrypting all communication between RADIUS servers, NAS devices, and cloud identity providers is essential to protect user credentials and session information. Secure transport mechanisms such as RadSec (RADIUS over TLS) or IPsec tunnels should be employed to safeguard traffic, especially when RADIUS servers are hosted outside the organization's trusted network or when requests traverse public cloud networks. Additionally, organizations must ensure that proper firewall rules, access controls, and certificate management practices are in place to minimize exposure to external threats.

Scalability is another major advantage of combining RADIUS with cloud authentication. Cloud-native identity platforms are designed to scale automatically to accommodate large numbers of users and requests, which complements the ability of RADIUS to handle high volumes of authentication traffic in distributed networks. By leveraging autoscaling capabilities of cloud RADIUS services or deploying additional RADIUS nodes in cloud environments, organizations can meet increased demand during peak usage periods or support expansion to new geographic locations.

Visibility and reporting are also enhanced through cloud integrations. Cloud identity providers often offer detailed audit logs, session insights, and compliance reporting tools that can be correlated with RADIUS accounting data. This enables security teams to have a unified view of user activity across network access points, cloud applications, and SaaS platforms. Integrating these logs with SIEM platforms or cloud-native security tools supports advanced threat detection, compliance audits, and incident response workflows.

Another trend in RADIUS and cloud authentication is the use of API-driven architectures. Modern cloud RADIUS solutions provide RESTful APIs that allow integration with custom applications, workflow automation tools, and orchestration platforms. Organizations can automate user provisioning, dynamically adjust access policies, or integrate RADIUS with security orchestration, automation, and response (SOAR) platforms to enhance operational efficiency and incident handling.

The shift to cloud authentication models has also introduced new identity federation scenarios where RADIUS is used in conjunction with identity brokers. Identity brokers act as intermediaries between the RADIUS infrastructure and multiple cloud identity providers, simplifying multi-cloud or multi-domain environments. For example, an organization operating in a merger or acquisition context may need to authenticate users across several identity platforms simultaneously. By leveraging an identity broker, RADIUS servers can route requests to the appropriate cloud provider, ensuring seamless authentication while maintaining centralized policy enforcement.

Ultimately, the integration of RADIUS with cloud authentication platforms bridges the gap between traditional AAA architectures and modern cloud-based identity ecosystems. This integration enables organizations to extend secure, policy-driven access control beyond the traditional enterprise perimeter, supporting remote workforces, hybrid networks, and cloud-hosted resources. As organizations continue to adopt cloud-first strategies, the demand for flexible and secure RADIUS and cloud authentication solutions will continue to grow, playing a vital role in the evolving landscape of network and identity management.

Federated Authentication and RADIUS

Federated authentication and RADIUS represent a powerful combination in modern network architectures, allowing organizations to extend their authentication capabilities across different administrative domains and service providers. Federated authentication enables users from one organization to securely access resources in another organization's network, without the need to create duplicate accounts or manage multiple identity stores. When combined with the RADIUS protocol, federated authentication becomes a scalable and standardized solution for implementing cross-domain network access in environments such as educational networks, public wireless access points, and partner organizations.

One of the most well-known examples of federated authentication using RADIUS is eduroam, the international federation that allows students, researchers, and faculty from participating institutions to access wireless networks at other member institutions using their home organization's credentials. This model relies on a hierarchical RADIUS infrastructure that includes local RADIUS servers at each organization, national RADIUS proxies, and global top-level RADIUS servers that route authentication requests based on domain information. The key benefit of this federated approach is that the user's home organization retains full control over the authentication process, ensuring that credentials never leave the trusted domain.

At the core of federated authentication with RADIUS is the concept of realm-based routing. When a user attempts to authenticate at a foreign organization, their request is sent to the local RADIUS server, which identifies the user's realm, typically defined as the domain part of the username (for example, user@university.edu). Based on this realm, the local RADIUS server forwards the authentication request to the next RADIUS proxy in the hierarchy, eventually reaching the home institution's RADIUS server. This home server validates the credentials and returns the appropriate access decision through the same proxy chain back to the originating NAS device.

Federated authentication using RADIUS introduces several technical and operational challenges. One of the most significant is ensuring consistent security policies and transport encryption across all participating RADIUS servers and proxies. As the authentication request may traverse multiple networks and intermediaries, it is essential to secure each hop using mechanisms such as RadSec (RADIUS over TLS) to prevent eavesdropping and man-in-the-middle attacks. Each RADIUS proxy must be configured to trust upstream and downstream servers through digital certificates, creating a trusted federation of nodes that enforce strong encryption and mutual authentication.

Policy enforcement is another critical aspect of federated authentication with RADIUS. The home organization defines the authentication policy, including whether to accept the login, apply multifactor authentication, or assign specific user roles. However, the visited organization also has the responsibility to enforce its local authorization policies, such as assigning users to guest VLANs, applying bandwidth restrictions, or limiting access to specific services. This dual-policy model allows both the home and visited institutions to maintain control over security and resource allocation, balancing user convenience with the need to protect network integrity.

Federated RADIUS environments often require careful configuration of RADIUS attributes to ensure interoperability. For example, certain attributes such as Filter-Id or Class may be included in Access-Accept responses from the home organization to influence how the visited network treats the user session. These attributes may define session time limits, VLAN assignments, or user privileges. Additionally, organizations participating in federations must agree on common attribute formats, naming conventions, and data validation practices to ensure smooth interoperation between different systems.

Accounting is another important component of federated RADIUS deployments. While authentication decisions are made by the user's home organization, accounting records must be generated and maintained by the visited organization's infrastructure. These records include session start and stop times, data usage, and other session-specific metrics. In some federated models, accounting information may be anonymized or aggregated before being shared with the home organization for reporting, billing, or statistical purposes. Ensuring the privacy and protection of accounting data is critical, particularly when dealing with regulations such as GDPR, which governs the handling of personal information across jurisdictions.

Scalability is a fundamental requirement in federated RADIUS infrastructures. As more organizations join the federation and as user numbers grow, the hierarchical RADIUS architecture must be capable of handling increased authentication traffic without introducing latency or bottlenecks. Load balancing, server clustering, and distributed proxy architectures are common strategies used to ensure that each layer of the hierarchy can manage authentication volumes efficiently. Geographically distributed top-level proxies also help to optimize routing paths and reduce the round-trip time between visited networks and home institutions.

Monitoring and incident response processes are critical in federated environments, where authentication issues may span multiple organizations. Federated RADIUS deployments often rely on collaborative monitoring platforms or shared troubleshooting tools to detect and resolve problems. Logs from local RADIUS servers, national proxies, and home institution servers must be analyzed collectively to pinpoint failures or misconfigurations. Frequent causes of issues include incorrect realm routing, misconfigured proxies, certificate trust chain errors, or timeouts due to network congestion.

Federated authentication using RADIUS is not limited to academic environments. Many corporations and public service organizations deploy federated models to support partnerships, roaming agreements, and multi-tenant environments. For example, global enterprises with multiple subsidiaries may implement a federated RADIUS architecture to enable seamless access to corporate Wi-Fi networks across different regional offices. Similarly, public Wi-Fi providers may partner with third-party identity providers to allow users to authenticate using credentials from social networks or external cloud identity services, with RADIUS serving as the intermediary protocol.

With the rise of cloud identity services, federated RADIUS environments are increasingly integrating with cloud-based identity providers. This hybrid approach enables users to authenticate with cloud credentials while still participating in traditional RADIUS-based federations. For example, an organization may configure its RADIUS servers to accept authentication requests from a federated partner and validate the credentials against a cloud identity platform using protocols such as SAML or OAuth2. This approach extends the reach of federated RADIUS networks to include cloud-native users and applications, supporting hybrid and multi-cloud strategies.

Security considerations are paramount in federated RADIUS deployments. Ensuring that all participating servers adhere to federation security policies, including the use of modern encryption standards and strict access controls, is essential to maintaining trust between members. Additionally, federated RADIUS infrastructures must implement incident response plans to address security breaches, service outages, or misconfigurations that could impact federation-wide operations.

Federated authentication and RADIUS enable organizations to create interconnected authentication ecosystems that facilitate seamless user access while maintaining centralized control and security. By leveraging the flexibility of RADIUS and the collaborative model of federated identity management, institutions and businesses can extend secure access to users across organizational boundaries, fostering greater cooperation and connectivity in today's distributed and dynamic IT landscape.

Advanced EAP Methods (EAP-TLS, EAP-TTLS, PEAP)

Advanced EAP methods, including EAP-TLS, EAP-TTLS, and PEAP, are integral to secure network authentication frameworks, providing enhanced protection for user credentials and network access control. These methods are part of the Extensible Authentication Protocol (EAP) family, which is widely used within RADIUS-based infrastructures to authenticate users on wireless and wired networks, as well as VPNs. Unlike legacy protocols such as PAP or CHAP, advanced EAP methods introduce strong encryption, mutual authentication, and tunneling capabilities to safeguard authentication exchanges from common threats such as eavesdropping, credential theft, and man-in-the-middle attacks.

EAP-TLS is considered one of the most secure and robust EAP methods available today. It is based on Transport Layer Security (TLS), the same protocol used to secure HTTPS web traffic. EAP-TLS uses digital certificates on both the client and the server to establish mutual authentication. During the authentication process, the client presents its certificate to the server, and the server presents its certificate to the client. If both certificates are valid and trusted, a secure TLS tunnel is established, and the client is granted access. The strength of EAP-TLS lies in its reliance on public key infrastructure (PKI) and the elimination of passwords, which are often the weakest link in authentication systems. By using certificates, organizations can ensure that only devices or users with valid credentials can access the network. EAP-TLS is frequently deployed in environments with stringent security requirements, such as government agencies, financial institutions, and large enterprises.

The deployment of EAP-TLS requires careful planning and management of digital certificates. Organizations must operate or integrate with a certificate authority (CA) to issue, revoke, and renew certificates for both RADIUS servers and client devices. Managing the certificate lifecycle is critical, as expired or improperly configured certificates can lead to authentication failures and service disruptions. Automated certificate management solutions or integrations with enterprise PKI systems help simplify this process and reduce administrative overhead. While EAP-TLS offers exceptional security, its complexity and management requirements have led some organizations to adopt other advanced EAP methods as alternatives.

EAP-TTLS (Tunneled Transport Layer Security) provides a flexible and secure alternative to EAP-TLS. Like EAP-TLS, EAP-TTLS establishes a TLS tunnel between the client and the server. However, EAP-TTLS only requires the server to present a certificate, while the client authenticates inside the tunnel using legacy methods such as PAP,

CHAP, or MS-CHAPv2. This approach allows organizations to leverage existing credential stores, such as LDAP directories or Active Directory, without issuing client-side certificates. EAP-TTLS is especially useful in environments where managing client certificates is impractical due to the diversity of devices or user populations, such as educational institutions or public hotspots.

Once the secure tunnel is established with EAP-TTLS, the client transmits its credentials securely to the server. This process ensures that sensitive information, such as passwords, is encrypted in transit and protected from eavesdropping or interception. EAP-TTLS supports a variety of inner authentication methods, providing flexibility for organizations to choose the most suitable method based on their security policies and infrastructure. Additionally, EAP-TTLS can support dynamic user or device profile assignments based on RADIUS attributes sent after successful authentication, enabling fine-grained access control.

PEAP (Protected Extensible Authentication Protocol) is another widely adopted advanced EAP method, designed to address similar concerns as EAP-TTLS but with stronger integration with Microsoft ecosystems. Like EAP-TTLS, PEAP creates a secure TLS tunnel between the client and the server, but the most common implementation uses MS-CHAPv2 as the inner authentication protocol. PEAP is favored in Windows-centric environments where Active Directory is the primary user directory and where native Windows supplicants can seamlessly integrate with PEAP authentication workflows.

The PEAP authentication process begins with the server presenting a digital certificate to the client, establishing a secure TLS tunnel. Once the tunnel is established, the client authenticates to the server by providing a username and password, which are typically validated against Active Directory or another directory service via the RADIUS server. Because the credentials are transmitted inside the encrypted tunnel, PEAP protects against credential theft and other common wireless threats. One of PEAP's advantages is its native support across many operating systems, particularly Microsoft Windows, which simplifies client-side configuration and reduces the need for third-party supplicants.

Despite their security benefits, all advanced EAP methods require proper configuration to be effective. A common pitfall is the use of weak or improperly managed server certificates. If clients are configured to ignore or bypass certificate validation, the security of the TLS tunnel is compromised, leaving the network vulnerable to rogue access points and man-in-the-middle attacks. Organizations must ensure that clients are configured to validate server certificates against trusted root CAs and that certificates are issued with appropriate validity periods, key lengths, and signature algorithms.

Performance considerations are also relevant when deploying advanced EAP methods. TLS handshakes and certificate validations introduce computational overhead for both clients and servers, which can impact authentication response times in large-scale environments. To mitigate this, administrators can enable session resumption features, such as TLS session tickets or TLS session IDs, which allow clients to reuse established TLS sessions for subsequent authentications, reducing the need for full handshakes on every connection attempt. This is particularly valuable in wireless environments where users frequently roam between access points.

Advanced EAP methods also play a key role in supporting enterprise mobility and BYOD policies. By enforcing EAP-TLS or PEAP authentication, organizations can ensure that only compliant devices are granted access to internal networks. Integration with mobile device management (MDM) platforms allows administrators to automate the distribution of configuration profiles and certificates to corporate-owned or personal devices, streamlining the onboarding process while maintaining security controls.

Another important consideration is compatibility across different client platforms. While modern operating systems and network devices generally support EAP-TLS, EAP-TTLS, and PEAP natively, certain legacy or specialized devices may lack support for specific methods. Organizations must assess their device inventory and user base to ensure that the selected EAP method is widely supported and aligns with their operational and security objectives.

Advanced EAP methods provide the foundation for secure and flexible network access control in diverse environments. Whether prioritizing the strong certificate-based authentication of EAP-TLS, the flexible tunneling approach of EAP-TTLS, or the Windows integration benefits of PEAP, organizations can deploy EAP solutions that meet their unique security, usability, and operational requirements. Each method enhances the security posture of the network by providing encrypted authentication exchanges and enabling granular access control policies via RADIUS integrations. As threats to network access continue to evolve, advanced EAP methods remain a critical component in safeguarding enterprise wireless and remote access infrastructures.

RADIUS Attributes for Advanced Control

RADIUS attributes are the key building blocks that enable advanced control over network access decisions. These attributes, defined as attribute-value pairs (AVPs), are exchanged between the RADIUS client (typically a Network Access Server or NAS) and the RADIUS server during authentication, authorization, and accounting transactions. The richness of the attribute framework within RADIUS allows administrators to implement fine-grained access control policies, dynamically assign network resources, and enforce security and compliance measures tailored to organizational needs.

When a RADIUS server responds to an Access-Request with an Access-Accept or Access-Reject message, it can include a variety of AVPs that determine how the NAS handles the user session. Among the most commonly used attributes for basic control are Service-Type, which defines the nature of the session (such as Login-User or Framed-User), and Framed-IP-Address, which specifies a static IP address assigned to the client. For enterprises and service providers managing large user populations or multiple service tiers, these attributes are essential in shaping how individual sessions are provisioned on the network.

A significant use case for advanced RADIUS attributes is dynamic VLAN assignment. By including the Tunnel-Type, Tunnel-Medium-Type, and Tunnel-Private-Group-ID attributes in the Access-Accept response, the RADIUS server can instruct a switch or wireless controller to place a user's session on a specific VLAN. This is particularly valuable in networks implementing role-based access control (RBAC), where employees, contractors, and guests must be segregated into different VLANs with distinct security and access policies. The ability to assign VLANs dynamically based on user group, department, or device type enhances network segmentation and reduces the risk of lateral movement by unauthorized users.

Bandwidth management is another area where RADIUS attributes provide advanced control. Attributes such as Filter-Id or vendor-specific attributes (VSAs) can define traffic shaping or rate-limiting policies to be applied by the NAS. For example, service providers offering multiple service tiers can configure their RADIUS server to return bandwidth profiles based on the user's subscription plan, ensuring that users receive the appropriate level of service without manual intervention on network equipment. This is commonly seen in ISP environments where residential users, business customers, and VIP clients may all access the same physical infrastructure but require differentiated treatment in terms of throughput and quality of service.

Session timeout and idle timeout attributes are critical for enforcing session duration policies. The Session-Timeout attribute allows administrators to define how long a user session can remain active before the NAS disconnects the user. This is useful in environments where session length must be limited for security or licensing reasons. The Idle-Timeout attribute, on the other hand, specifies the maximum idle time (no user activity) before a session is terminated. These attributes help organizations optimize resource utilization, enforce compliance with access policies, and reduce the likelihood of abandoned or dormant sessions consuming network resources unnecessarily.

The Class attribute is often used to carry information about the user session that can be referenced later during accounting or for policy enforcement. This attribute can hold identifiers that track session state, user profiles, or other metadata. It is commonly used in conjunction with centralized policy servers or external AAA frameworks that require session correlation for post-authentication decision-making or reporting. Similarly, the Reply-Message attribute can be used to deliver custom messages to end users upon successful or failed authentication, providing an opportunity to communicate policy reminders, usage restrictions, or other contextual information.

Advanced control also comes into play when integrating RADIUS with multi-factor authentication (MFA) solutions. Certain attributes can be utilized to enforce step-up authentication based on specific conditions, such as the user's role, device posture, or geographic location. For instance, users authenticating from outside the corporate network or using untrusted devices may be directed to an MFA challenge, while internal users on managed devices might only be required to complete primary authentication. This conditional enforcement is enabled by combining RADIUS attributes with external policy engines or identity platforms that evaluate contextual data and dynamically determine the appropriate access flow.

Vendor-Specific Attributes (VSAs) are an essential mechanism for implementing device- or vendor-specific controls beyond the standard RADIUS attribute set. Network equipment manufacturers often define their own VSAs to enable proprietary features, such as advanced QoS settings, custom access control lists (ACLs), or device-specific monitoring capabilities. By returning VSAs in the RADIUS response, administrators can fine-tune the behavior of network devices to enforce highly customized policies. For example, a wireless LAN controller from one vendor may support a proprietary VSA to assign a user to a specific wireless QoS profile based on their RADIUS group membership.

Accounting attributes also play a vital role in advanced control scenarios. Attributes such as Acct-Input-Octets, Acct-Output-Octets, and Acct-Session-Time provide detailed insights into user behavior and session consumption. This data can be used for post-session analysis, regulatory compliance, or billing purposes. In service provider environments, accounting data may be processed in near real-time to trigger actions such as disconnecting a user who exceeds a data cap or applying usage-based charges.

Security enforcement can be further enhanced by combining RADIUS attributes with network enforcement points. For instance, integration with Network Access Control (NAC) systems allows RADIUS attributes to carry device posture information, such as the presence of up-to-date antivirus software, operating system versions, or encryption status. Based on this information, the RADIUS server can instruct the NAS to quarantine non-compliant devices by assigning them to a remediation

VLAN, limiting their network access until security requirements are met.

RADIUS attributes also facilitate integration with identity and access management (IAM) solutions. By passing attributes that map to user roles, departments, or other directory-based identifiers, RADIUS can act as a bridge between IAM systems and network enforcement devices. This integration allows for centralized policy management while enabling dynamic, real-time enforcement at the network edge. For example, a user's Active Directory group membership can determine their VLAN assignment, access to specific applications, or priority in bandwidth allocation.

Another area where RADIUS attributes are used for advanced control is in mobile and IoT device management. Mobile devices and IoT endpoints often lack traditional user interfaces for complex authentication methods. Using MAC authentication bypass (MAB) in conjunction with RADIUS attributes, network administrators can control access for these devices based on MAC address whitelisting and assign appropriate network policies. By dynamically applying VLANs, ACLs, and session timeouts based on device type or profile, administrators can securely onboard and manage non-user-driven endpoints.

In summary, the extensive and flexible use of RADIUS attributes enables organizations to implement advanced access control strategies across a wide range of network environments. From dynamic VLAN assignments and bandwidth policies to session management and integration with external security tools, RADIUS attributes are the foundation for creating intelligent, context-aware network access solutions that align with both operational needs and security requirements. As networks become more dynamic and user populations more diverse, the role of RADIUS attributes in shaping network access and enforcing business logic will continue to expand, offering organizations powerful tools to manage access in increasingly complex environments.

Customizing Vendor-Specific Attributes (VSAs)

Customizing Vendor-Specific Attributes (VSAs) is a crucial capability within RADIUS environments, allowing organizations to leverage proprietary features of network devices and tailor access control decisions to meet complex business and technical requirements. While the RADIUS protocol defines a standard set of attributes used across vendors for common authentication, authorization, and accounting functions, many network hardware and software vendors extend this functionality through their own custom attribute sets, referred to as VSAs. These attributes enable the application of unique configurations or enforcement mechanisms that are specific to a particular brand or product line, providing greater flexibility in managing network behavior.

VSAs are identified by a vendor-specific identifier, which corresponds to the vendor's unique code as assigned by the Internet Assigned Numbers Authority (IANA). When a RADIUS server responds to an Access-Request message with an Access-Accept, Access-Reject, or Access-Challenge, it can include VSAs designed to trigger specific features or actions on the NAS device, such as wireless controllers, VPN gateways, or switches. By customizing these attributes, administrators can deliver highly granular access policies tailored to the capabilities and requirements of the deployed hardware.

One common use case for customizing VSAs is in wireless network deployments. Different wireless LAN controller vendors provide unique VSAs that allow administrators to control advanced settings, such as assigning users to specific wireless QoS profiles, controlling session timeouts, or applying device-specific roaming optimizations. For instance, one vendor's VSA may enable dynamic VLAN pooling or fast-roaming features for mobile users, while another may allow the application of custom access control lists (ACLs) directly from the RADIUS server. These features are not always achievable using the standard RADIUS attribute set, making VSAs indispensable in fine-tuning wireless network performance and security.

VPN concentrators and remote access solutions also rely heavily on VSAs to extend functionality. Vendors often implement VSAs to define virtual routing and forwarding (VRF) instances, policy-based routing rules, or advanced bandwidth control measures that are not available through standard RADIUS attributes. In these environments, a RADIUS server may return VSAs specifying the VPN tunnel group, encryption domain, or split-tunneling policies, influencing how the VPN appliance establishes and secures user sessions. Customizing VSAs in this context allows for dynamic application of VPN policies based on user roles, group membership, or other directory-based attributes.

Another prominent application of customized VSAs is in service provider networks. ISPs and telecommunications providers frequently use VSAs to implement differentiated service levels based on customer profiles. For example, certain VSAs may define download and upload rate limits, burst rates, or queuing strategies enforced by the access router or BRAS. Through dynamic assignment of these attributes, ISPs can enforce traffic shaping policies aligned with service-level agreements (SLAs), offering tiered service plans to customers while automating enforcement through the RADIUS infrastructure.

The customization process of VSAs begins with understanding the specific requirements of the network deployment and the features available on the target NAS devices. Vendors typically document their VSA sets, including the attribute names, associated values, and expected behaviors when these attributes are applied. RADIUS server administrators must translate these requirements into appropriate configurations within the server's policy framework. In open-source RADIUS servers such as FreeRADIUS, this involves editing configuration files to define policies that trigger the inclusion of specific VSAs in the server's response based on user identity, group, NAS IP address, or other conditions.

Testing and validation are key components of customizing VSAs effectively. Since VSAs operate beyond the standard RADIUS framework, incorrect formatting or misapplied attributes may result in unintended behavior on NAS devices. For example, an incorrectly configured QoS profile VSA could result in degraded network performance or policy violations. Administrators should thoroughly test VSA configurations in staging or lab environments before deploying them into production. Logs from both the RADIUS server and the NAS device are essential in troubleshooting issues, as they can reveal how attributes are parsed and whether they are applied as intended.

Customizing VSAs is also instrumental in implementing advanced security controls. Network vendors often introduce security-focused VSAs to enable capabilities such as dynamic ACL enforcement, device fingerprinting, or posture-based access control. For example, certain switches or wireless controllers can apply ACLs returned via VSAs to limit a user's access to specific IP subnets, services, or applications. This dynamic security model enhances network segmentation and mitigates threats by ensuring that users are only granted the minimum level of access required for their roles or devices.

Scalability is another benefit of customizing VSAs. Rather than configuring static policies on each individual NAS device, administrators can centralize control by dynamically assigning VSAs via the RADIUS server. This approach reduces administrative overhead and simplifies policy management across large, distributed networks. Changes to access control policies, VLAN assignments, or QoS profiles can be made at the RADIUS server level, automatically propagating to all NAS devices as users authenticate, ensuring consistency across the environment.

Interoperability is a key consideration when customizing VSAs, particularly in multi-vendor environments. Each vendor defines VSAs according to its own specifications, and these attributes are typically not compatible across different product lines. Administrators must ensure that VSAs returned to a specific NAS device match that device's expected vendor format. This often requires creating conditional logic within the RADIUS server configuration to detect the NAS identifier or vendor type and return the correct set of VSAs accordingly. In FreeRADIUS, this can be accomplished using unlang policy language to create conditional statements based on the NAS-IP-Address or NAS-Identifier attributes.

Documentation and version control are critical in environments where customized VSAs play a significant role. Network and security teams must maintain detailed records of VSA configurations, including their intended purpose, applied values, and associated vendor documentation. Version control systems can help track changes to RADIUS policies and VSA assignments, providing a clear audit trail and facilitating rollback in the event of configuration errors or policy shifts.

As network technologies evolve, vendors continue to expand their VSA offerings to support emerging capabilities, such as software-defined networking (SDN), IoT security, and cloud-integrated access control. Staying informed about updates to VSA documentation and software releases is essential for administrators to fully leverage the potential of customized VSAs in modern networks.

Customizing Vendor-Specific Attributes is a powerful tool for extending the capabilities of RADIUS beyond its standard framework. By enabling granular control over network devices and tailoring access and service policies to specific business needs, VSAs play a pivotal role in creating flexible, efficient, and secure network access solutions. Whether enhancing wireless performance, enforcing differentiated service tiers, or applying dynamic security measures, VSAs provide the adaptability needed to meet the growing demands of today's complex IT infrastructures.

Mobile Device Authentication via RADIUS

Mobile device authentication via RADIUS has become a central component in securing modern enterprise networks, particularly as organizations embrace bring-your-own-device (BYOD) policies and expand their mobile workforce. With the proliferation of smartphones, tablets, and laptops accessing corporate networks both on-premises and remotely, ensuring secure, reliable authentication for these devices is critical. RADIUS serves as the backbone of network access control for mobile devices, providing centralized authentication, dynamic authorization, and accounting capabilities across wireless, wired, and VPN environments.

Mobile device authentication typically occurs in wireless networks where users connect via Wi-Fi using 802.1X and Extensible

Authentication Protocol (EAP) methods supported by the RADIUS server. The authentication process begins when a mobile device, acting as the supplicant, initiates a connection to the wireless network. The wireless access point or controller, acting as the Network Access Server (NAS), forwards the authentication request to the RADIUS server, which then verifies the user's identity and enforces access control policies.

One of the most secure methods for authenticating mobile devices via RADIUS is the use of EAP-TLS. This protocol relies on mutual certificate-based authentication, where both the RADIUS server and the mobile device present valid digital certificates before establishing a secure TLS tunnel. EAP-TLS ensures that only trusted devices with properly issued certificates can access the network, significantly reducing the risk of unauthorized access. Organizations implementing mobile device management (MDM) or enterprise mobility management (EMM) solutions often automate the distribution of certificates to managed devices, streamlining the onboarding process while maintaining strong security controls.

In environments where managing client certificates is impractical, other EAP methods such as PEAP-MSCHAPv2 or EAP-TTLS can be employed to authenticate mobile devices using username and password credentials. These methods encapsulate credentials within an encrypted TLS tunnel, protecting them from interception over untrusted wireless networks. Mobile devices configured with corporate credentials can authenticate to the RADIUS server via these secure tunnels, ensuring that user identities are validated before network access is granted.

Mobile device authentication via RADIUS also supports dynamic authorization, allowing administrators to assign access rights based on user roles, device posture, or contextual information such as time of day or location. Through RADIUS attribute-value pairs (AVPs), the RADIUS server can instruct the wireless controller or access point to apply specific policies during session establishment. For example, corporate-owned mobile devices may be placed into a secure VLAN with full internal network access, while BYOD devices are dynamically assigned to a restricted VLAN that only provides internet connectivity.

This dynamic control improves network segmentation and helps enforce compliance with corporate security policies.

Accounting is another essential feature provided by RADIUS during mobile device authentication. Each session initiated by a mobile device generates RADIUS accounting messages, including session start and stop records, session duration, and data usage metrics. These records can be integrated with network monitoring tools or security information and event management (SIEM) platforms to provide visibility into mobile device activity on the network. By analyzing accounting logs, administrators can detect unusual patterns, such as devices consuming excessive bandwidth or accessing the network during non-business hours, which may indicate policy violations or security incidents.

Mobile devices also present unique challenges in RADIUS-based authentication workflows. Due to their portability, mobile devices frequently roam between access points, leading to session reauthentication events. To minimize user disruption and enhance the user experience, organizations can enable features such as fast roaming (802.11r) or pre-authentication mechanisms supported by both wireless infrastructure and RADIUS servers. These optimizations reduce authentication latency and ensure seamless transitions as mobile users move throughout the physical environment.

The diversity of mobile device operating systems adds another layer of complexity to RADIUS deployments. Android, iOS, Windows, and other platforms each have specific requirements and limitations regarding EAP method support, certificate handling, and supplicant configurations. Ensuring consistent and secure RADIUS authentication across a heterogeneous device landscape requires careful planning, user training, and, where possible, the deployment of configuration profiles or mobile device management policies. These tools help automate the setup of Wi-Fi profiles, including network SSIDs, EAP settings, and certificate trust chains, reducing the likelihood of misconfigurations that could compromise security.

RADIUS servers must also integrate with identity management systems to authenticate mobile devices effectively. In most organizations, mobile users' credentials are stored in directory services such as Active

Directory or cloud identity providers. The RADIUS server queries these directories via LDAP, Kerberos, or other protocols to validate user credentials during the authentication process. In hybrid environments, the RADIUS server may act as a bridge between on-premises and cloud identity sources, enabling mobile devices to authenticate regardless of their location or the identity platform managing user accounts.

Security hardening is critical when authenticating mobile devices via RADIUS. Wireless networks are inherently more exposed than wired environments, making them attractive targets for attackers seeking to intercept or spoof authentication traffic. To mitigate these risks, administrators must enforce strong encryption protocols, such as WPA2-Enterprise or WPA3-Enterprise, and ensure that RADIUS communications with the NAS are secured via shared secrets or encrypted transport mechanisms like RadSec. Additionally, configuring mobile devices to validate server certificates during the EAP handshake is essential to prevent man-in-the-middle attacks using rogue access points.

The rise of zero trust network access (ZTNA) strategies has further elevated the role of RADIUS in mobile device authentication. Within a zero trust framework, every device, including mobile endpoints, must continuously prove its identity and security posture before and during network access. RADIUS integrates with network access control (NAC) systems and posture assessment tools to evaluate mobile device compliance in real time. Devices that fail security checks, such as missing security patches or lacking endpoint protection, may be denied access or placed into a remediation network segment.

RADIUS authentication also supports the implementation of multi-factor authentication (MFA) for mobile devices. While EAP-TLS provides certificate-based device authentication, additional factors, such as one-time passwords (OTP) or push notifications from mobile authenticator apps, can be integrated into the workflow. For instance, a user attempting to connect to a corporate Wi-Fi network may first authenticate their device via EAP-TLS, followed by a second factor delivered through a cloud-based MFA service before gaining full network access. This layered approach significantly enhances security by addressing threats associated with compromised credentials or stolen devices.

As organizations continue to adopt remote and hybrid work models, the demand for secure mobile device authentication via RADIUS will grow. Employees working from home or connecting from public hotspots rely on VPN services secured by RADIUS-based authentication workflows. In such scenarios, the RADIUS server not only authenticates the device but also enforces security policies such as split tunneling, session timeouts, or IP filtering through returned attributes to the VPN concentrator.

Mobile device authentication via RADIUS remains a critical component of enterprise network security. By providing centralized authentication, dynamic access control, and comprehensive accounting for mobile endpoints, RADIUS enables organizations to manage the challenges of mobile connectivity while maintaining robust security postures. As mobile threats and device diversity continue to evolve, organizations must continuously refine their RADIUS deployments, integrating with modern identity platforms, enforcing advanced security policies, and supporting seamless, user-friendly access to corporate resources.

RADIUS and Multi-Factor Authentication (MFA)

RADIUS and Multi-Factor Authentication (MFA) are a powerful combination that enhances the security of enterprise networks by introducing an additional layer of protection beyond traditional username and password authentication. As cyber threats become more sophisticated and credential theft remains a prevalent attack vector, relying solely on single-factor authentication methods is no longer sufficient to protect critical infrastructure and sensitive data. By integrating RADIUS with MFA solutions, organizations can implement strong authentication mechanisms across VPNs, wireless networks, wired infrastructure, and cloud services, reinforcing access controls and reducing the risk of unauthorized entry.

The integration of MFA with RADIUS typically works by augmenting the standard authentication process with one or more secondary verification steps, such as one-time passwords (OTPs), push notifications, hardware tokens, biometric verification, or out-of-band communication. When a user initiates an authentication request, for example, by connecting to a VPN or Wi-Fi network, the NAS forwards the credentials to the RADIUS server. The RADIUS server, acting as an authentication gateway, validates the primary credentials and triggers an MFA challenge through the configured MFA provider.

One of the most common scenarios is the use of RADIUS with OTP-based MFA systems. These systems generate time-sensitive codes that users must enter in addition to their username and password. Solutions like Google Authenticator, Microsoft Authenticator, or hardware tokens from vendors such as RSA SecureID or YubiKey can be integrated into the RADIUS authentication flow. After validating the user's credentials against a backend directory such as LDAP or Active Directory, the RADIUS server queries the MFA system to verify the OTP provided by the user. Only after successful completion of both factors does the RADIUS server return an Access-Accept response to the NAS.

Push-based MFA is another widely adopted method, particularly valued for its user convenience and strong security. When a user attempts to authenticate, the MFA provider sends a push notification to the user's registered mobile device. The user must approve the request to complete the authentication. This method reduces reliance on manual entry of OTPs and streamlines the user experience while maintaining high security standards. RADIUS servers integrated with cloud-based MFA providers such as Duo Security, Okta Verify, or Azure MFA can seamlessly support push notifications, adding flexibility to network access control.

A critical consideration when deploying RADIUS with MFA is the user experience and the balance between security and convenience. Organizations must decide when and where to enforce MFA policies. Some deployments apply MFA universally across all access requests, while others implement conditional access rules based on contextual data such as user roles, device compliance status, location, or time of day. By integrating RADIUS with policy engines or identity platforms, organizations can dynamically determine which sessions require MFA and which can rely on primary authentication alone. For example, employees accessing the corporate network from a managed device within the office may bypass the MFA prompt, while remote users connecting from untrusted networks are required to complete an MFA challenge.

RADIUS servers can be configured to enforce MFA through various methods depending on the deployment model. Some organizations integrate MFA directly within the RADIUS server using plugins or modules that communicate with the MFA system. Open-source RADIUS servers like FreeRADIUS support custom scripts, PAM modules, or API calls to external MFA services. Alternatively, some environments utilize an MFA proxy server that sits between the NAS and the backend identity provider, intercepting RADIUS requests and handling MFA challenges before forwarding them to the RADIUS server.

The accounting and logging capabilities of RADIUS are critical when implementing MFA. Every authentication attempt, whether successful or failed, generates detailed records that include timestamps, usernames, NAS identifiers, and authentication outcomes. These logs are essential for security audits, incident investigations, and regulatory compliance. Integrating RADIUS logs with SIEM platforms allows organizations to detect patterns such as repeated failed MFA attempts, which could indicate credential stuffing or brute-force attacks targeting the secondary factor.

Securing RADIUS communication channels is vital when deploying MFA, as sensitive authentication traffic, including MFA-related data, passes through these channels. Organizations must ensure that RADIUS messages are encrypted using RadSec or IPsec tunnels, especially when NAS devices and RADIUS servers communicate across untrusted networks or cloud environments. Additionally, securing the communication between the RADIUS server and the MFA provider via HTTPS, mutual TLS, or VPN tunnels ensures that secondary factor verifications remain protected from interception or tampering.

MFA integration with RADIUS is particularly valuable in VPN deployments, where remote users require secure access to internal systems and applications. VPN concentrators configured as RADIUS clients can enforce MFA by forwarding user credentials to the RADIUS server, which in turn challenges users with an additional factor before granting access. This layered approach helps prevent attackers from exploiting stolen credentials to gain remote access, a tactic frequently observed in cyberattacks targeting corporate networks.

Wireless networks also benefit from RADIUS and MFA integration. Users connecting to enterprise Wi-Fi networks using 802.1X authentication can be required to complete an MFA challenge during the EAP authentication process. This is especially useful for organizations implementing BYOD policies, as it ensures that personal devices connecting to internal networks meet the same strong authentication requirements as corporate-managed endpoints. By combining RADIUS, EAP methods such as PEAP or EAP-TTLS, and MFA, organizations can enforce secure, certificate-based or password-based authentication augmented with a secondary verification step.

As organizations adopt cloud and hybrid infrastructures, MFA integrated with RADIUS extends to cloud-hosted services and SaaS applications. Cloud-based RADIUS servers or RADIUS-as-a-Service offerings often provide built-in MFA capabilities or native integrations with leading cloud identity providers. This enables consistent enforcement of MFA policies across both on-premises and cloud resources, simplifying identity and access management while improving the organization's overall security posture.

Automation and orchestration also play a key role in scaling MFA with RADIUS in large environments. By leveraging APIs provided by modern MFA vendors, organizations can automate the enrollment and deprovisioning of users, manage MFA tokens or devices, and streamline administrative tasks related to MFA policy enforcement. This reduces operational overhead and ensures that MFA processes remain efficient and scalable as the user base grows.

Ultimately, the integration of RADIUS and Multi-Factor Authentication provides organizations with a comprehensive framework for securing network access and defending against credential-based attacks. By adding an additional layer of verification, MFA significantly raises the difficulty for threat actors attempting to compromise user accounts, even if primary credentials are stolen or leaked. The flexibility of RADIUS, combined with the evolving capabilities of modern MFA platforms, allows enterprises to implement tailored security strategies that balance protection, usability, and operational efficiency in dynamic IT environments.

Integrating RADIUS with Single Sign-On (SSO)

Integrating RADIUS with Single Sign-On (SSO) provides a unified and seamless authentication experience for users while maintaining the centralized control and security benefits of RADIUS. As organizations increasingly adopt cloud-based applications, hybrid infrastructures, and distributed workforces, the demand for SSO grows. SSO allows users to authenticate once and gain access to multiple systems, services, and applications without the need to re-enter their credentials for each resource. By combining SSO with RADIUS, organizations can extend this convenience and security model to network access control systems such as VPNs, Wi-Fi networks, and wired networks that rely on RADIUS for AAA (Authentication, Authorization, and Accounting) services.

The traditional RADIUS model authenticates users against backend identity stores such as LDAP directories or Active Directory. However, in modern environments, many organizations have shifted to cloud identity providers that manage users through SSO platforms, including Azure Active Directory, Okta, Ping Identity, or Google Workspace. These identity providers often serve as the primary authentication authority across multiple applications and services. By integrating RADIUS with SSO, organizations enable their users to authenticate to network services using the same credentials and session tokens they use for cloud applications and web-based portals.

One approach to achieving this integration is through the use of SSO-to-RADIUS gateways or proxies. These intermediary systems act as translators, bridging the gap between the RADIUS protocol and modern SSO protocols such as SAML, OpenID Connect (OIDC), or OAuth2. When a user attempts to authenticate to a network resource such as a VPN or wireless network, the NAS forwards the authentication request to the RADIUS server. The RADIUS server, in turn, redirects or forwards the authentication flow to the SSO gateway. The gateway handles the SSO process by directing the user to their identity provider for authentication. Once authenticated, the SSO gateway translates the SSO assertion into a RADIUS Access-Accept response and passes it back to the RADIUS server, completing the authentication cycle.

Another model involves directly integrating the RADIUS server with APIs provided by the SSO platform. In this architecture, the RADIUS server acts as a client to the SSO identity provider, querying it to validate tokens or session data during the RADIUS authentication process. This tighter integration reduces latency and complexity, as the RADIUS server can directly validate SSO tokens without relying on additional intermediaries. It also allows for dynamic policy enforcement, where the RADIUS server can request additional claims or attributes from the SSO platform to apply context-aware access control decisions based on user roles, device posture, or risk levels.

Integrating RADIUS with SSO streamlines the user experience significantly. Users no longer need to manage separate sets of credentials for VPNs, wireless networks, or other RADIUS-secured services. Instead, the same login session used for accessing cloud applications can also grant network access, reducing friction and improving productivity. This is particularly valuable in organizations with remote or hybrid workforces that frequently transition between corporate applications and secure network services.

Security is a core benefit of integrating RADIUS with SSO. Modern SSO platforms enforce strong authentication policies, such as multifactor authentication (MFA), adaptive risk-based authentication, and device trust validation. When integrated with RADIUS, these protections extend to network access points, reducing the risk of unauthorized access through compromised credentials. For example, a user connecting to a corporate VPN would be required to complete an MFA challenge through the SSO provider before being granted access, even if the VPN is using a legacy RADIUS-based authentication mechanism.

The integration also supports federated identity models. In multi-organization environments, users from trusted external domains can authenticate to network services through their home identity providers using federation protocols supported by the SSO platform. The SSO-to-RADIUS gateway or integrated RADIUS server can validate these federated assertions and issue RADIUS access responses, allowing seamless cross-organizational access without requiring local user accounts in the RADIUS server or NAS devices.

An important consideration when integrating RADIUS with SSO is session management and token lifecycle control. SSO platforms typically issue tokens with defined expiration times and session parameters. The RADIUS infrastructure must be configured to handle token validation consistently with the organization's session policies. For instance, when a user authenticates to a VPN using an SSO-issued token, the VPN session timeout enforced by the NAS should align with the validity period of the token or the user's SSO session. In cases where token refresh or reauthentication is required, integration with the SSO provider's API ensures that tokens are validated in real time against current session states.

Dynamic authorization is another advantage of combining RADIUS with SSO. Many SSO platforms provide rich attribute data and claims about users, including group memberships, department codes, or device compliance status. By passing these attributes to the RADIUS server during authentication, administrators can enforce granular network access policies. For example, users in the finance department may be granted access to a specific VLAN with additional controls, while contractors or guest users are assigned to isolated segments with restricted internet-only access. The RADIUS server can dynamically return these policies to the NAS based on the SSO-provided data.

The flexibility of RADIUS and SSO integration extends to compliance and auditability. RADIUS accounting logs can be enriched with session metadata obtained from the SSO platform, providing a comprehensive record of authentication events and user activity across both network and application layers. This integration supports regulatory requirements such as those outlined in PCI DSS, HIPAA, or ISO/IEC 27001, by ensuring that network access control is fully aligned with centralized identity governance frameworks.

As organizations increasingly transition to cloud-native architectures, RADIUS and SSO integration plays a vital role in bridging legacy authentication systems with modern identity management platforms. By leveraging SSO for initial authentication while maintaining RADIUS for network-level access enforcement, organizations gain the best of both worlds—seamless user experiences and strong network security.

To implement this integration effectively, organizations must carefully assess compatibility between their existing RADIUS infrastructure and their chosen SSO provider. Not all NAS devices or VPN appliances natively support SSO protocols, making the use of SSO-to-RADIUS gateways or API integrations necessary. Proper planning, testing, and user training are essential to ensure that the integrated solution works consistently across different device types and access scenarios, from corporate laptops to mobile devices connecting over public Wi-Fi.

Ultimately, integrating RADIUS with Single Sign-On allows organizations to unify network and application authentication workflows under a single, centralized identity framework. This approach enhances security, simplifies identity management, and improves the overall user experience across diverse access channels. As SSO platforms continue to evolve with new capabilities such as passwordless authentication and conditional access, their integration with RADIUS infrastructures will remain a key strategy for organizations seeking to modernize their security and access control ecosystems.

API-Driven RADIUS Implementations

API-driven RADIUS implementations represent a modern approach to managing and extending RADIUS functionality in dynamic, automated network environments. As organizations shift towards DevOps practices, cloud-native infrastructures, and agile development cycles, the need for flexible and programmable RADIUS integrations has grown. Traditional RADIUS deployments rely heavily on static configuration files and manual management, which can limit responsiveness to business needs and complicate the integration of RADIUS into larger network automation workflows. By introducing

APIs to interact with RADIUS servers or their supporting systems, administrators gain the ability to automate tasks, enforce dynamic policies, and streamline operations at scale.

An API-driven RADIUS implementation typically leverages RESTful APIs to interact with external components such as identity providers, configuration management systems, orchestration platforms, and policy engines. These APIs allow RADIUS servers to retrieve user data, apply custom logic, or dynamically modify authentication and authorization decisions based on real-time information. Instead of relying solely on static user databases or directory lookups, API-driven models make RADIUS servers part of a broader, programmable security and access control framework.

A common use case for API-driven RADIUS is dynamic policy enforcement based on external identity attributes or risk assessments. For example, when a user attempts to authenticate to a network via RADIUS, the server can query an external policy engine or identity management system through an API to retrieve additional context about the user. This could include group memberships, geolocation data, device compliance status, or even a real-time risk score calculated by a security information and event management (SIEM) system. Based on this external data, the RADIUS server can adjust its authorization response dynamically, such as placing the user into a restricted VLAN, triggering multi-factor authentication, or applying specific bandwidth policies. This level of integration provides organizations with highly granular and adaptive access control capabilities.

API-driven architectures are also critical for supporting dynamic environments where user roles, access requirements, and network configurations change frequently. In cloud-native or software-defined networking (SDN) environments, for example, network segments, virtual appliances, and service endpoints are often provisioned or decommissioned automatically based on workload demands. By integrating RADIUS with orchestration tools such as Ansible, Terraform, or Kubernetes through APIs, administrators can ensure that RADIUS policies and configurations are updated in real time to reflect changes in the network topology or user population. This helps prevent inconsistencies between the RADIUS infrastructure and the evolving network landscape.

Automation of routine tasks is another benefit of API-driven RADIUS implementations. Tasks such as user provisioning, onboarding, and revocation can be automated by connecting RADIUS servers to identity and access management (IAM) platforms or human resources systems via APIs. For instance, when a new employee is added to an organization's HR system, an automated workflow could create the corresponding user account in the directory, enroll the user in the appropriate RADIUS policies, and assign them to the correct VLAN or role-based access control (RBAC) group. Similarly, when an employee leaves the organization, API calls can trigger immediate deprovisioning of the user's access within the RADIUS server, reducing the risk of orphaned accounts and potential security breaches.

API-driven RADIUS also enables seamless integration with modern security platforms such as Zero Trust Network Access (ZTNA) solutions and Secure Access Service Edge (SASE) architectures. These models rely heavily on context-aware policies that adapt to user behavior, device posture, and other dynamic factors. By exposing APIs, RADIUS servers can communicate directly with cloud-based security platforms to exchange authentication logs, receive risk-based policy decisions, or participate in automated incident response actions. For example, if a SIEM system detects suspicious activity associated with a user, it could call the RADIUS API to quarantine the user's session by reassigning them to a remediation VLAN or triggering a session termination.

API-driven RADIUS deployments also provide a foundation for self-service portals and user-driven workflows. Organizations can build custom portals where users request network access, register devices, or manage authentication tokens. These portals communicate with the RADIUS backend via APIs to perform actions such as device registration, certificate enrollment, or retrieval of access credentials. By empowering users with self-service capabilities, organizations can reduce help desk ticket volume and improve operational efficiency while maintaining centralized control over access policies.

Another critical advantage of API-driven RADIUS implementations is enhanced monitoring and observability. By exposing APIs for log retrieval, status checks, and performance metrics, RADIUS servers can integrate with modern observability tools and dashboards. This integration enables real-time visibility into authentication trends, server health, and policy enforcement outcomes. Administrators can automate alerting workflows based on metrics such as failed login rates, unusual traffic patterns, or system resource utilization, allowing for faster detection and remediation of performance issues or security incidents.

Security is paramount in API-driven RADIUS environments. All APIs exposed by the RADIUS server or associated components must be secured using industry best practices, including HTTPS encryption, token-based authentication, and role-based access control. API endpoints should be designed with the principle of least privilege in mind, ensuring that only authorized applications and users can perform sensitive operations such as modifying policies or terminating sessions. Additionally, API activity should be logged and monitored to detect unauthorized access attempts or misuse.

API-driven RADIUS implementations also enable tighter integration with DevOps pipelines. Infrastructure-as-code (IaC) principles can be extended to the RADIUS infrastructure, allowing network access policies to be version-controlled, tested, and deployed as part of automated CI/CD workflows. This ensures that RADIUS configurations remain consistent across development, staging, and production environments and that any changes to access policies undergo rigorous testing and approval processes before being rolled out.

As enterprise networks continue to evolve toward automation, cloud adoption, and dynamic security models, API-driven RADIUS implementations offer a future-proof solution for integrating traditional AAA services with modern IT ecosystems. By extending RADIUS capabilities beyond static configuration files and enabling dynamic interaction with external platforms, APIs empower organizations to create flexible, scalable, and highly secure network access control systems. This approach aligns with contemporary demands for agility, resilience, and operational efficiency, positioning API-enabled RADIUS as a key enabler in the modern cybersecurity and network management landscape.

Transitioning to Diameter Protocol

Transitioning to Diameter protocol represents a strategic evolution for organizations seeking to modernize their authentication, authorization, and accounting (AAA) infrastructure. Diameter was designed as a successor to RADIUS, addressing several limitations found in traditional RADIUS environments while introducing enhanced security, scalability, and flexibility for contemporary network demands. As networks have grown more complex and applications have shifted to IP-based services with increasingly dynamic requirements, Diameter has emerged as a robust solution to meet these evolving needs, particularly in large-scale telecommunications, LTE networks, and next-generation IP multimedia systems.

The decision to transition from RADIUS to Diameter is often driven by the need for improved protocol capabilities. While RADIUS remains widely used and is sufficient for many enterprise use cases, it has inherent limitations such as relying on the connectionless and unreliable UDP transport layer. Diameter, in contrast, operates over TCP or Stream Control Transmission Protocol (SCTP), offering reliable delivery of AAA messages with built-in error handling and congestion control mechanisms. This shift to a reliable transport protocol enhances the robustness of Diameter-based deployments, reducing the risk of lost packets or authentication delays caused by network congestion or unreliable links.

Diameter introduces native support for end-to-end security features through IPsec and TLS, addressing one of RADIUS's major shortcomings regarding encryption and message integrity. While RADIUS encrypts only specific fields such as passwords, leaving other portions of the payload exposed, Diameter offers comprehensive security at the transport layer. This provides organizations with greater confidence in protecting AAA traffic from eavesdropping, tampering, and replay attacks, especially when authentication transactions traverse untrusted networks or service provider domains.

Another key advantage of transitioning to Diameter is its improved extensibility and flexibility in supporting complex network architectures. Diameter defines a modular framework with multiple applications, allowing it to address use cases beyond simple network access control. For example, Diameter can be used to support mobility management, policy and charging control, and session handling in LTE and 5G networks. Its ability to carry a broader set of attributes and service-specific parameters makes Diameter an ideal choice for service providers implementing advanced policy control and billing scenarios that would be difficult to manage within the constraints of traditional RADIUS AVPs.

The transition process from RADIUS to Diameter requires careful planning to minimize disruption and ensure compatibility with existing systems. One of the first steps is assessing the current network infrastructure to identify which components rely on RADIUS for AAA functionality. These components may include wireless controllers, VPN concentrators, DSL access servers, and NAS devices. Many of these legacy systems may lack native Diameter support, necessitating the use of protocol translation or interworking functions. Diameter-RADIUS gateways are often deployed to bridge this gap, translating RADIUS messages to Diameter format and vice versa, allowing organizations to introduce Diameter into the network without requiring a full replacement of existing RADIUS-compatible devices.

A crucial consideration during this transition is the redesign of AAA server configurations. While RADIUS and Diameter share conceptual similarities, such as exchanging authentication requests and responses, their message structures, attribute handling, and session management mechanisms differ significantly. Diameter supports richer message sets and more complex transaction models, including stateful sessions and error reporting. Organizations must ensure that Diameter configurations reflect these capabilities, taking advantage of Diameter's ability to negotiate capabilities between peers, define session timeouts dynamically, and provide detailed error diagnostics.

Diameter's peer-to-peer communication model, in contrast to the client-server model commonly associated with RADIUS, also impacts deployment architecture. In Diameter, peers establish relationships based on a common Diameter identity and exchange messages directly, often using Diameter agents or relay nodes to manage routing, load balancing, and failover. This model promotes more efficient and resilient network designs but may require organizations to re-architect parts of their AAA infrastructure to align with Diameter's routing and session management paradigms.

Transitioning to Diameter also demands updates to security and compliance frameworks. The use of TLS and IPsec for securing Diameter traffic must be integrated into existing security policies, including key and certificate management processes. Organizations should enforce mutual authentication between Diameter peers, implement strong cryptographic standards, and ensure compliance with regulations governing the handling of authentication data. Additionally, security monitoring tools and SIEM platforms must be configured to ingest and analyze Diameter logs, which may contain different message types and attributes than those typically found in RADIUS accounting records.

Training and knowledge transfer are essential during the transition to Diameter. Network and security teams must develop a deep understanding of Diameter's architecture, message flows, and configuration practices. This includes learning how to interpret Diameter-specific attributes, troubleshoot peer-to-peer communication issues, and configure Diameter routing agents to ensure optimal performance and redundancy. Proper documentation and operational procedures should be established to support ongoing maintenance and incident response activities in the Diameter environment.

The transition to Diameter often coincides with broader network modernization initiatives. For telecommunications providers, Diameter plays a central role in the evolution towards IP Multimedia Subsystem (IMS) architectures and 5G core networks. In these contexts, Diameter enables interoperability between critical network elements such as Policy and Charging Rules Functions (PCRF), Home Subscriber Servers (HSS), and Mobility Management Entities (MME). The ability of Diameter to support advanced signaling and policy control functions makes it indispensable in delivering differentiated services, enforcing quality of service (QoS) policies, and enabling seamless user mobility across network domains.

For enterprise networks, transitioning to Diameter may be less common but is still relevant for organizations that require tighter integration with mobile networks or are building infrastructure that must interoperate with carrier-grade systems. In such cases, Diameter's support for advanced authentication scenarios, including enhanced session management and attribute handling, can provide value in high-performance or mission-critical environments.

As the transition progresses, organizations should establish a phased migration plan, starting with deploying Diameter infrastructure components in parallel with existing RADIUS systems. Testing interoperability between legacy and Diameter-compatible systems is vital to ensure smooth service continuity. Over time, as network devices and services are upgraded or replaced with Diameter-capable alternatives, the reliance on RADIUS can be reduced, and the network can fully leverage the benefits offered by Diameter.

Ultimately, transitioning to Diameter is a strategic decision that enables organizations to modernize their AAA systems and prepare for the demands of next-generation network services. By adopting Diameter, organizations gain a more secure, extensible, and reliable framework for managing authentication, authorization, and accounting across diverse and complex network architectures. The success of the transition depends on meticulous planning, investment in staff training, and the deployment of appropriate tools and processes to support the evolving AAA landscape.

Comparing RADIUS and TACACS+

Comparing RADIUS and TACACS+ requires a deep understanding of the two protocols and their respective roles within network security and access control frameworks. Both RADIUS (Remote Authentication Dial-In User Service) and TACACS+ (Terminal Access Controller Access Control System Plus) are AAA protocols designed to provide authentication, authorization, and accounting services. However, their design philosophies, transport mechanisms, and primary use cases diverge significantly. Organizations evaluating these protocols must consider how each aligns with their network architecture, security requirements, and administrative needs.

RADIUS, originally designed to manage user access for dial-up services, has since become the dominant AAA protocol for wireless networks, VPNs, and many wired network environments. It operates over UDP, prioritizing speed and efficiency, which makes it well-suited for high-volume authentication tasks such as managing thousands of wireless or remote user sessions. RADIUS has become the industry standard for client-server communication in wireless LAN authentication via 802.1X, as well as for securing VPN access where fast session establishment is critical.

TACACS+, by contrast, is more frequently used for controlling administrative access to network infrastructure devices such as routers, switches, and firewalls. It was developed by Cisco as a replacement for the earlier TACACS and XTACACS protocols and is widely supported across enterprise-grade networking equipment. Unlike RADIUS, TACACS+ operates over TCP, which provides reliable transport and ensures that packets are delivered in order without loss. This reliability is especially valuable in device management contexts where command authorization and logging need to be tightly controlled and fully auditable.

A key differentiator between the two protocols lies in how they handle AAA functions. RADIUS combines authentication and authorization into a single process. When a user requests access, the RADIUS server responds with both an authentication decision and a set of authorization parameters, such as assigned VLANs or session timeouts, in one transaction. This approach is efficient for use cases like Wi-Fi access or VPN connections, where users are primarily requesting access to network resources rather than executing administrative commands.

TACACS+, on the other hand, separates authentication, authorization, and accounting into discrete processes. This separation allows for more granular control over each phase of access. For example, TACACS+ can authenticate a network administrator when they log into a device, authorize specific commands they are allowed to run on that device, and account for each command execution individually. This capability is essential for organizations with strict security policies and compliance requirements, as it enables detailed control and auditing of administrative actions performed on critical network infrastructure.

Another fundamental difference is how each protocol secures transmitted data. RADIUS only encrypts the password within the Access-Request packet, while the rest of the message, including username and attribute data, is left in plaintext. Although this has traditionally been mitigated by deploying RADIUS over IPsec or RadSec (RADIUS over TLS), the protocol's native security is relatively limited. TACACS+, by design, encrypts the entire payload of its messages, including usernames, passwords, and authorization data. This comprehensive encryption provides enhanced confidentiality and is a significant factor for organizations prioritizing end-to-end security of management traffic.

In terms of deployment scenarios, RADIUS is commonly found in enterprise wireless networks, public Wi-Fi hotspots, and ISP environments where the focus is on authenticating end users and managing their access to network resources. RADIUS integrates well with identity management systems such as LDAP directories or Active Directory, allowing users to authenticate to network services using existing corporate credentials. It is also widely supported by a variety of NAS devices, including wireless controllers, VPN concentrators, and remote access servers, making it a versatile solution for user-facing authentication needs.

TACACS+ is favored in network operations centers and data centers where managing administrative access to routers, switches, and firewalls is a top priority. Network administrators often use TACACS+ to implement role-based access control (RBAC) for IT staff, defining which commands specific users or groups can execute on particular devices. For example, a junior network engineer may be granted read-only access to configuration files, while a senior engineer may have full administrative privileges to modify routing tables or interface settings. This level of control is difficult to achieve with RADIUS, which typically grants or denies access as a binary decision without command-level granularity.

Accounting features also differ between the two protocols. RADIUS accounting focuses on session-level data, recording when a user starts and ends a session, how much data was transferred, and other session-specific metrics. This information is valuable for usage reporting, billing in ISP environments, and compliance auditing in enterprise networks. TACACS+ accounting is more focused on administrative actions, logging each command entered on a network device, along with the username and timestamp associated with each action. This detailed command-level logging is essential for forensic investigations and for meeting compliance standards that require a full audit trail of administrative activities.

From a scalability perspective, both protocols are capable of handling large environments when properly architected. RADIUS servers can be configured in redundant and load-balanced clusters to support millions of authentication requests across distributed network environments. Similarly, TACACS+ can be deployed in highly available configurations to support thousands of network devices and administrative users. However, the decision to deploy one protocol over the other often depends on the nature of the devices being protected and the type of access being controlled.

Vendor support is another factor influencing protocol choice. While RADIUS enjoys universal support across most networking equipment, including wireless access points, VPN gateways, and firewalls, TACACS+ support is somewhat more specialized. Cisco equipment offers native TACACS+ support, and many other enterprise networking vendors have adopted the protocol in recognition of its popularity within Cisco-centric environments. Nevertheless, RADIUS maintains broader adoption due to its role in user authentication for diverse access scenarios.

Ultimately, RADIUS and TACACS+ are not mutually exclusive. Many organizations deploy both protocols concurrently to address distinct requirements. RADIUS secures user access to wireless and remote networks, while TACACS+ governs administrative access to the infrastructure itself. This dual-protocol approach allows organizations to leverage the strengths of each protocol, providing comprehensive control over both user and device-level security. Selecting the appropriate protocol, or combination thereof, requires a detailed analysis of organizational needs, compliance obligations, and network architecture, ensuring that AAA functions are optimized for performance, security, and administrative efficiency.

RADIUS Security Best Practices

RADIUS security best practices are critical for safeguarding authentication, authorization, and accounting processes in modern networks. As RADIUS is frequently deployed to control access to wireless networks, VPNs, wired infrastructure, and other critical network resources, ensuring that RADIUS deployments are configured with security in mind is essential to defending against unauthorized access, data breaches, and service disruptions. While RADIUS is a mature and widely adopted protocol, it has several inherent limitations, particularly in how it handles encryption and data confidentiality, that require careful mitigation through proper design, configuration, and operational practices.

One of the most fundamental best practices in securing a RADIUS environment is enforcing strong shared secrets between RADIUS clients, such as Network Access Servers (NAS) or VPN concentrators, and RADIUS servers. These shared secrets are used to encrypt sensitive parts of the RADIUS packet, such as the user password, using the MD5 hash function. Weak or reused shared secrets increase the risk of successful brute-force attacks or replay attacks, especially if traffic is intercepted. Organizations should generate long, random, and complex shared secrets for each RADIUS client and rotate them regularly as part of their security hygiene.

Encrypting the entire RADIUS communication channel is also a critical step in mitigating risks associated with RADIUS's native security limitations. While RADIUS encrypts only the password field, all other attributes, including usernames and session data, are sent in plaintext. This exposes sensitive information to potential interception if traffic crosses untrusted networks. Implementing IPsec or RadSec (RADIUS over TLS) ensures that all RADIUS communications are protected at the transport layer, providing confidentiality, integrity, and authentication of messages. Deploying RADIUS over encrypted tunnels is particularly important in environments where RADIUS messages traverse public networks or are exchanged between geographically distributed sites.

Limiting network exposure is another key practice for securing RADIUS infrastructure. Administrators should implement strict network segmentation, ensuring that only trusted NAS devices and management workstations can communicate with the RADIUS servers. Firewalls should be configured to permit RADIUS traffic on UDP port 1812 (authentication) and UDP port 1813 (accounting) exclusively from authorized IP addresses. Employing access control lists (ACLs) on network devices further reduces the attack surface, blocking unauthorized devices from sending RADIUS requests or attempting to scan RADIUS services.

Hardening the RADIUS server itself is essential to maintaining a secure deployment. This includes applying the principle of least privilege, ensuring that the RADIUS service runs with only the minimum permissions required to function correctly. Regularly updating the RADIUS server software to the latest version helps protect against known vulnerabilities. Administrators should also disable or remove any unused modules or plugins that could introduce unnecessary attack vectors. Where possible, RADIUS servers should be dedicated to their role, minimizing the risk of cross-service vulnerabilities by avoiding the installation of unrelated applications or services on the same system.

Logging and monitoring play a central role in RADIUS security best practices. RADIUS servers should be configured to generate detailed logs of authentication attempts, including successful logins, failed attempts, and accounting events. These logs provide valuable insight into potential security incidents, such as brute-force attacks, unauthorized access attempts, or credential misuse. Integrating RADIUS logs with a centralized Security Information and Event Management (SIEM) platform allows for real-time correlation and alerting, enabling security teams to respond quickly to suspicious activity. Logs should be protected from tampering through appropriate file permissions and, where necessary, secure transmission to off-site log servers.

Another key practice is enforcing robust authentication policies that go beyond simple username and password verification. RADIUS servers should integrate with identity management systems capable of supporting multi-factor authentication (MFA) for all user access requests. Whether users are authenticating to a corporate Wi-Fi network or connecting to a VPN, adding an additional factor such as a one-time password (OTP), push notification, or biometric verification significantly reduces the risk of unauthorized access resulting from compromised credentials. Modern RADIUS servers and cloud-based identity providers make it straightforward to enforce MFA policies as part of the authentication workflow.

Granular authorization is equally important when designing secure RADIUS policies. RADIUS responses should include attribute-value pairs (AVPs) that dynamically assign users to specific network segments or VLANs based on their role, device type, or security posture. For example, guest devices can be directed to isolated VLANs with limited internet access, while employees are placed on corporate VLANs with access to internal resources. Dynamic assignment enhances security by preventing lateral movement from less trusted users or devices to sensitive parts of the network. In environments with network access control (NAC) systems, posture assessment results can be incorporated into RADIUS policies, allowing devices that fail security checks to be quarantined automatically.

Redundancy and high availability are also integral to RADIUS security planning. A single point of failure in the authentication infrastructure can disrupt user access to critical resources. Organizations should deploy RADIUS servers in redundant configurations, often using load balancers or NAS-level failover mechanisms to distribute authentication and accounting requests across multiple servers. Redundancy ensures continuity of service during maintenance windows or unexpected outages and prevents attackers from targeting a single RADIUS node to cause a denial-of-service (DoS) scenario.

Administrators must also ensure that RADIUS configurations align with broader organizational security policies and regulatory requirements. This includes implementing secure password policies, maintaining audit logs for compliance audits, and following industry standards such as ISO/IEC 27001 or NIST guidelines for AAA infrastructure. In environments subject to regulatory frameworks such as PCI DSS, HIPAA, or GDPR, special attention must be paid to how authentication data is handled, transmitted, and retained.

Periodic vulnerability assessments and penetration testing should be conducted on RADIUS infrastructure to identify misconfigurations or weaknesses that could be exploited by attackers. This includes testing for common issues such as weak shared secrets, open RADIUS ports exposed to the internet, and insecure NAS configurations. Findings from these assessments should inform remediation efforts and the continuous improvement of RADIUS security practices.

Lastly, organizations should invest in training network and security teams on RADIUS best practices, including secure deployment, hardening techniques, and troubleshooting authentication issues. Teams should understand the nuances of RADIUS packet structures, common attack vectors such as replay attacks and credential guessing, and how to use RADIUS debug logs to investigate authentication anomalies.

A secure RADIUS deployment is not a one-time task but a continuous process of review, monitoring, and enhancement. By following these security best practices, organizations can protect their network authentication infrastructure, mitigate risks, and ensure the confidentiality and integrity of user access processes across wireless networks, VPNs, and enterprise systems. A well-secured RADIUS environment serves as a foundational element of a broader network security strategy, supporting the organization's efforts to protect its assets and users from evolving cybersecurity threats.

Future Trends in RADIUS Technology

Future trends in RADIUS technology are shaped by the evolving landscape of enterprise networking, cloud computing, zero trust architectures, and the need for scalable, secure, and programmable authentication systems. While RADIUS has remained a fundamental component of network security for decades, its future is being influenced by the growing complexity of modern IT environments and the demand for tighter integration with emerging identity and access management frameworks. As networks continue to expand beyond traditional perimeters, RADIUS is adapting to support new security models, automation workflows, and hybrid infrastructures.

One significant trend is the integration of RADIUS with zero trust network access (ZTNA) architectures. In a zero trust model, every user, device, and application must be continuously verified and authenticated regardless of location or network segment. RADIUS is playing a crucial role in extending zero trust principles to network access layers, especially in wireless and VPN environments. Future RADIUS deployments will increasingly leverage dynamic policy enforcement driven by external policy engines or security orchestration platforms. By incorporating contextual information such as device health, user behavior, and location, RADIUS servers will deliver more adaptive access decisions, supporting the shift from static perimeter defenses to identity-centric security.

Another emerging trend is the growing adoption of RADIUS in cloud-native and multi-cloud environments. As enterprises migrate critical workloads and applications to the cloud, RADIUS is being integrated with identity-as-a-service (IDaaS) platforms and cloud-based directory services. RADIUS-as-a-Service offerings are becoming more common, providing organizations with managed AAA solutions that eliminate the need for maintaining on-premises RADIUS infrastructure. These cloud-native RADIUS platforms are designed to integrate seamlessly with cloud identity providers, such as Azure Active Directory, Okta, and Google Workspace, enabling unified authentication workflows across on-premises networks, cloud resources, and SaaS applications.

The use of RADIUS over secure transport protocols like RadSec is also gaining traction. As awareness of RADIUS's inherent security limitations grows, more organizations are adopting RADIUS over TLS (RadSec) to encrypt all RADIUS traffic, protecting sensitive authentication data and mitigating the risk of interception or manipulation. Future RADIUS deployments are likely to standardize RadSec as a baseline security requirement, particularly in distributed environments where authentication requests traverse untrusted networks. Additionally, improvements in TLS performance and the widespread availability of cloud-based certificate management services are making RadSec implementations easier to deploy and manage.

API-driven RADIUS implementations are reshaping how organizations interact with and automate their AAA services. As IT teams increasingly embrace DevOps principles, RADIUS servers are being enhanced with RESTful APIs that enable dynamic provisioning of users, automation of policy changes, and integration with infrastructure-as-code pipelines. This trend supports agile development practices, allowing network teams to deploy RADIUS configurations alongside application and network updates in CI/CD workflows. The ability to programmatically manage RADIUS policies and configurations will become a standard feature in future RADIUS implementations, reducing operational overhead and aligning AAA services with modern automation frameworks.

Integration with artificial intelligence (AI) and machine learning (ML) is expected to influence RADIUS technology as organizations look to enhance real-time threat detection and dynamic risk assessment. By feeding RADIUS authentication data into AI-powered security platforms, organizations can gain deeper insights into user behavior, detect anomalies, and adjust access policies dynamically. For example, if a user's authentication patterns suddenly deviate from established baselines, the RADIUS server could trigger additional security controls such as multi-factor authentication or quarantine actions. This level of intelligence will elevate RADIUS beyond a simple AAA mechanism to a key component of adaptive and context-aware security ecosystems.

Another future trend is the evolution of RADIUS to support identity federation and cross-domain authentication more effectively. While RADIUS proxies and federation models like eduroam currently facilitate inter-organizational authentication, future RADIUS systems are expected to offer tighter integration with federated identity protocols such as SAML and OpenID Connect. This will enable seamless single sign-on experiences across multiple organizations and service providers, reducing authentication friction while preserving centralized control over security policies. As organizations increasingly participate in collaborative networks and service provider ecosystems, federated RADIUS capabilities will become essential for ensuring secure and scalable access control.

Scalability and high availability will remain a focus area for RADIUS technology, particularly as enterprises and service providers seek to support growing user bases and expanding device ecosystems. Future RADIUS servers will incorporate advanced load-balancing algorithms, distributed architectures, and microservices-based designs to handle millions of concurrent authentication requests with minimal latency. The rise of edge computing will also influence RADIUS scalability, with organizations deploying lightweight RADIUS components at edge locations to authenticate users closer to the network perimeter while maintaining centralized policy management.

RADIUS technology is also being adapted to better support the Internet of Things (IoT). As IoT devices proliferate across industries, the need for secure, scalable, and automated onboarding mechanisms has intensified. RADIUS will increasingly integrate with IoT onboarding protocols and device identity management systems, enabling dynamic policy enforcement based on device types, security postures, or manufacturing data. This evolution will ensure that IoT devices can be authenticated and segmented securely, mitigating the risks associated with unsecured or misconfigured endpoints in smart buildings, manufacturing plants, and critical infrastructure.

As organizations place greater emphasis on user privacy and regulatory compliance, RADIUS systems will evolve to support stronger data protection features. Future RADIUS implementations will provide enhanced logging and auditing capabilities to meet the demands of compliance frameworks such as GDPR, HIPAA, and PCI DSS. This includes anonymizing sensitive user data in logs, encrypting stored authentication records, and integrating with compliance reporting tools. Additionally, RADIUS solutions will likely incorporate more granular access controls for administrators, ensuring that AAA system configurations and logs are accessible only to authorized personnel in line with regulatory requirements.

Finally, the future of RADIUS will be influenced by its coexistence and potential convergence with Diameter and other next-generation AAA protocols. While Diameter is often deployed in telecom and mobile carrier networks due to its advanced capabilities, RADIUS continues to dominate in enterprise and ISP environments. However, as organizations seek unified AAA platforms that can serve both legacy and modern systems, hybrid solutions supporting both RADIUS and Diameter protocols may emerge. These solutions will enable gradual transitions to more advanced AAA frameworks while maintaining backward compatibility with existing RADIUS-dependent devices and applications.

As networks continue to evolve and security requirements become more complex, RADIUS technology will remain a foundational element of AAA services, adapting to meet the demands of next-generation access control, automation, and security frameworks. Its continued evolution will ensure that RADIUS remains relevant and capable in supporting secure, scalable, and flexible network authentication across a wide range of use cases and industries.

Case Studies of RADIUS Deployments

RADIUS has been deployed across a wide variety of industries and environments to address authentication, authorization, and accounting requirements. Examining real-world case studies provides valuable insights into how organizations leverage RADIUS to secure their networks, enhance user experience, and achieve compliance. Each deployment offers different challenges and lessons, depending on the scale, industry, and specific business needs of the organization.

One example of a successful RADIUS deployment is a multinational financial institution that needed to unify its access control systems across regional offices worldwide. The organization operated hundreds of branch locations, each with its own legacy authentication system, creating inconsistency and security gaps across the network. By deploying a centralized RADIUS infrastructure with redundant servers located in multiple global data centers, the institution was able to enforce a single, cohesive access policy for employees, contractors, and remote workers. The RADIUS servers were integrated with the corporate Active Directory environment to ensure that user identities and group memberships were reflected in the authentication process. To secure traffic between branch offices and the data centers, RADIUS traffic was encapsulated in IPsec tunnels. Additionally, the institution implemented dynamic VLAN assignments using RADIUS attribute-value pairs to ensure users were automatically placed into the appropriate network segment based on their department or role. This deployment resulted in a significant reduction in administrative overhead and improved compliance with financial industry regulations requiring strict control over internal network access.

A different use case involved a large university that needed to provide secure and seamless Wi-Fi access to tens of thousands of students, faculty, and visitors across a sprawling campus. The university implemented a RADIUS-based 802.1X wireless authentication system integrated with its student information system and employee directory. To address the challenge of onboarding personal devices in a BYOD environment, the university deployed a self-service portal that allowed users to configure their devices with the correct 802.1X settings and certificates, all backed by the RADIUS infrastructure. The RADIUS servers were configured to assign users to VLANs based on their affiliation, with students, faculty, staff, and guests receiving different levels of network access. For visitors from partner institutions, the university participated in the eduroam federation, leveraging its RADIUS proxy capabilities to forward authentication requests to external identity providers. The result was a seamless roaming experience for visiting researchers and students, while local users benefited from secure, encrypted wireless access. This deployment significantly improved network security by eliminating the use of open Wi-Fi networks and ensured that every connected device was authenticated against a trusted identity source.

In the telecommunications sector, a major internet service provider (ISP) implemented RADIUS to manage authentication and accounting for its broadband subscribers. The ISP provided DSL and fiber services to residential and business customers, and it needed a scalable AAA infrastructure capable of handling millions of daily authentication requests. The ISP deployed multiple geographically distributed RADIUS servers in active-active configurations, ensuring high availability and load balancing across its network. These servers authenticated PPPoE sessions initiated by customer-premises equipment (CPE) and returned service-specific authorization parameters, such as bandwidth limits and IP address assignments, based on the customer's subscription plan. Accounting data collected by RADIUS was integrated with the ISP's billing system to generate monthly invoices. The ISP also implemented RADIUS proxy functionality to route authentication requests from third-party resellers to the appropriate backend servers, enabling a wholesale model that supported multiple brands under the same infrastructure. This large-scale deployment enabled the ISP to deliver reliable internet services while maintaining tight control over user access, bandwidth allocation, and customer billing.

A healthcare organization provides another compelling case study. With multiple hospitals and clinics under its umbrella, the organization faced the challenge of securing its internal wireless networks to protect sensitive patient information. Using RADIUS in conjunction with 802.1X authentication and EAP-TLS, the organization ensured that only devices with valid digital certificates could access the internal network. Certificates were distributed to corporate-managed laptops, mobile devices, and medical equipment through an enterprise mobility management (EMM) platform. The RADIUS servers interfaced with an LDAP directory that provided information about device ownership and user roles, enabling the assignment of devices to secure VLANs with access to patient care systems and medical records. Guest devices, including those used by patients and visitors, were placed into an isolated VLAN with internet-only access. The healthcare provider also configured RADIUS to integrate with a security information and event management (SIEM) system, allowing real-time monitoring of authentication attempts and generating alerts for suspicious behavior such as repeated authentication failures or unusual connection patterns. This deployment improved compliance with healthcare regulations, such as HIPAA, and reduced the risk of unauthorized access to critical patient data.

In the public sector, a government agency responsible for national transportation infrastructure implemented RADIUS to secure remote access to its internal networks. The agency's field engineers, who worked at remote sites, required VPN access to connect to internal systems and applications. The agency deployed RADIUS to authenticate VPN sessions initiated through IPsec tunnels and integrated it with a multi-factor authentication system that required users to enter a one-time password delivered through a secure mobile application. The RADIUS server validated user credentials against the agency's Active Directory and then forwarded OTPs to the external MFA provider through an API. Only after successful completion of both factors would the RADIUS server issue an Access-Accept response. By adding this second layer of authentication, the agency significantly improved the security of its remote access infrastructure, protecting critical operational technology (OT) systems from unauthorized access and potential cyberattacks.

In each of these case studies, RADIUS proved to be a versatile and reliable protocol for addressing a wide range of authentication and access control challenges. Whether supporting wireless networks in educational environments, managing customer accounts in service provider networks, or enforcing regulatory compliance in healthcare and government sectors, RADIUS provides the flexibility and scalability necessary for modern network security. Organizations continue to rely on RADIUS not only for its core AAA functionality but also for its ability to integrate with other technologies, such as VPNs, identity directories, MFA platforms, and SIEM solutions. These real-world examples highlight the enduring relevance of RADIUS as a foundational component of network access security across diverse industries and use cases.

Common Pitfalls and How to Avoid Them

Deploying and managing a RADIUS infrastructure presents several challenges that organizations frequently encounter. While RADIUS is a mature and widely adopted protocol, its versatility and complexity can lead to misconfigurations and oversights if best practices are not followed. Common pitfalls in RADIUS deployments can undermine security, reduce performance, and lead to operational inefficiencies. By understanding these challenges in depth, network and security teams can implement strategies to avoid them and maintain a resilient and secure RADIUS environment.

One of the most frequent pitfalls in RADIUS implementations is the use of weak or poorly managed shared secrets between RADIUS clients and servers. The shared secret is a critical security element that protects sensitive data such as passwords by encrypting them within the RADIUS packet. Many organizations overlook the importance of generating strong, random shared secrets and instead reuse the same secret across multiple clients or use easily guessable strings. This exposes the system to brute-force attacks and could allow attackers to spoof NAS devices or decrypt authentication traffic. Avoiding this pitfall requires creating unique, complex secrets for each NAS device and enforcing a periodic secret rotation policy to reduce the risk of long-term exposure.

Another common issue is the failure to properly secure RADIUS traffic. By default, RADIUS operates over UDP, and while it encrypts the password field, other information like usernames and session attributes are sent in plaintext. Organizations often deploy RADIUS over unencrypted links, especially when traffic crosses different sites or cloud environments, leaving authentication data vulnerable to interception. To prevent this, administrators should adopt secure transport mechanisms such as IPsec or RadSec, which encrypt the entire RADIUS communication. Ensuring that RADIUS traffic is confined to trusted networks and protected by firewalls or access control lists is also essential to minimizing the attack surface.

Misconfigured authentication policies present another significant pitfall. Some deployments rely on overly permissive or poorly defined policies that do not adequately differentiate between user roles, devices, or security posture. For example, granting all users the same VLAN assignment or network privileges regardless of their role or location creates unnecessary risk and weakens network segmentation. To address this, organizations should leverage RADIUS attribute-value pairs to enforce dynamic policies based on contextual data, such as user groups, device types, or time-of-day rules. Implementing role-based access control (RBAC) within the RADIUS infrastructure ensures that users are granted only the minimum access necessary for their roles.

An often-overlooked issue is the lack of redundancy and high availability in RADIUS deployments. Some organizations deploy a single RADIUS server without considering failover scenarios, leaving the network vulnerable to service outages if the server experiences downtime or performance degradation. RADIUS is a mission-critical service, especially in environments where it supports wireless access or VPN authentication for remote users. To avoid this pitfall, administrators should deploy RADIUS servers in redundant configurations, either through active-active load balancing or active-passive failover setups. Ensuring that NAS devices are configured with multiple RADIUS server IPs further mitigates the risk of a single point of failure.

Poor integration with identity management systems is another challenge. Organizations often integrate RADIUS with external directories such as LDAP or Active Directory without optimizing queries or properly managing the directory structure. This can result in slow authentication response times and increased load on the directory servers. Issues such as unindexed LDAP attributes or inefficient query filters can significantly affect performance. Avoiding this requires reviewing and optimizing directory schemas, indexing commonly queried attributes, and tuning RADIUS server configurations to limit unnecessary query depth or scope.

Logging misconfigurations can hinder incident response and compliance efforts. In some environments, logging is disabled or configured at insufficient verbosity levels, leaving gaps in audit trails and making it difficult to diagnose authentication failures or security incidents. In contrast, enabling overly verbose logging in high-traffic environments can flood log storage systems and obscure actionable insights. To avoid this pitfall, organizations should establish a balanced logging strategy, ensuring that critical events such as authentication attempts, failures, and accounting records are captured and forwarded to a centralized logging platform. Integrating logs with a SIEM system enhances visibility and supports automated detection of anomalies, such as repeated failed login attempts or rogue devices attempting to authenticate.

Failing to regularly update and patch RADIUS servers is another pitfall that can expose organizations to known vulnerabilities. Outdated software may contain security flaws that attackers can exploit to bypass authentication, gain unauthorized access, or disrupt services. Many organizations operate legacy RADIUS implementations that have not been updated due to concerns over compatibility or a lack of awareness of available patches. Addressing this issue involves establishing a proactive patch management process, testing updates in controlled environments before production rollout, and subscribing to vendor or open-source project mailing lists to stay informed of security advisories.

Improper load balancing and resource allocation can lead to performance bottlenecks in large-scale RADIUS deployments. In high-demand environments such as ISPs or large enterprises with thousands of concurrent users, a single RADIUS server or under-provisioned virtual machine may struggle to process requests in a timely manner. This can result in slow authentication times, session drops, or even service outages during peak periods. To mitigate this, administrators should implement horizontal scaling strategies by distributing RADIUS workloads across multiple servers and load balancers. Monitoring system resources, such as CPU and memory usage, allows teams to identify capacity limits and provision additional resources before they impact performance.

Inconsistent configurations between RADIUS servers in redundant or distributed environments can create operational headaches and security risks. When RADIUS nodes operate with diverging policies, shared secrets, or integration settings, users may experience inconsistent behavior depending on which server handles their authentication request. For example, one server may enforce a stricter MFA policy than another, creating confusion and gaps in enforcement. This pitfall can be avoided by using configuration management tools, such as Ansible or Puppet, to standardize and automate RADIUS configuration across all servers in the deployment.

Finally, neglecting user education and support is a frequent source of friction in RADIUS-based environments. When users are unfamiliar with secure authentication processes, such as configuring 802.1X supplicants on personal devices or responding to MFA prompts during RADIUS authentication, help desk teams may face increased support requests and users may adopt insecure workarounds. Clear communication, user-friendly onboarding portals, and well-documented setup guides are essential for ensuring that end-users can comply with security policies without disrupting productivity.

Avoiding these common pitfalls requires a combination of technical rigor, proactive monitoring, and operational discipline. By addressing these areas systematically, organizations can maximize the reliability, security, and efficiency of their RADIUS deployments, ensuring that their network access control infrastructure supports both business objectives and evolving cybersecurity requirements.

RADIUS Reference and Resources

RADIUS Reference and Resources form a critical foundation for professionals seeking to implement, maintain, and enhance Remote Authentication Dial-In User Service infrastructures. The protocol, originally defined in RFC 2865, is well-documented through official standards, vendor-specific guidelines, and a wealth of open-source community contributions. Understanding and accessing these references ensures that network and security teams are equipped with the knowledge required to design robust authentication, authorization, and accounting solutions that meet both operational and security requirements.

The cornerstone of RADIUS documentation begins with the Internet Engineering Task Force (IETF) Request for Comments (RFC) publications. RFC 2865 serves as the primary document defining the core functionality of RADIUS, detailing how Access-Request, Access-Accept, Access-Reject, and other essential messages are formatted and processed. RFC 2866 focuses on RADIUS accounting, describing how to track session start and stop times, data usage, and other metrics vital to auditing and billing processes. RFC 2867 provides specifications for RADIUS accounting over reliable transport protocols, while RFC 5080 outlines security considerations and best practices for hardening RADIUS environments against common attack vectors. Collectively, these documents provide the technical blueprint for deploying standards-compliant RADIUS solutions.

For organizations implementing advanced features, additional RFCs such as RFC 3579 and RFC 3580 offer crucial insights. RFC 3579 specifies how Extensible Authentication Protocol (EAP) is encapsulated within RADIUS, enabling support for secure authentication methods like EAP-TLS and PEAP. RFC 3580 addresses the integration of RADIUS with IEEE 802.1X, a critical requirement for deploying secure wired and wireless network access. Further, RFC 6613 introduces RadSec, or RADIUS over TLS, providing guidance on securing RADIUS communications across public or untrusted networks by leveraging encrypted transport channels.

Open-source communities have also produced valuable resources for RADIUS practitioners. FreeRADIUS, one of the most widely used open-source RADIUS servers, maintains extensive documentation and a collaborative support community. The FreeRADIUS website hosts configuration guides, module references, troubleshooting tips, and comprehensive tutorials covering topics such as dynamic VLAN assignment, policy scripting using unlang, and integration with external databases like MySQL and PostgreSQL. Additionally, FreeRADIUS forums, mailing lists, and GitHub repositories are active with contributions from developers and users who share configuration examples, patches, and automation tools that streamline RADIUS management.

Many network equipment vendors publish RADIUS implementation guides tailored to their platforms. Cisco, Juniper, Aruba, and other networking vendors provide detailed technical documents explaining how to configure NAS devices, VPN concentrators, and wireless controllers to function as RADIUS clients. These vendor-specific resources often include step-by-step procedures for enabling RADIUS authentication, integrating with LDAP or Active Directory, customizing vendor-specific attributes (VSAs), and troubleshooting common issues related to device-RADIUS communication. These documents are indispensable when deploying RADIUS in heterogeneous network environments that include equipment from multiple vendors.

Beyond technical standards and vendor documentation, several books serve as comprehensive references for RADIUS administrators. Titles such as "RADIUS: Securing Public Access to Private Resources" by Jonathan Hassell and "Network Security with OpenSSL" provide both foundational knowledge and practical insights into secure authentication architectures. These books often cover topics such as cryptography principles related to RADIUS, integration of RADIUS with PKI systems for certificate-based authentication, and real-world deployment scenarios. For advanced users, in-depth exploration of authentication protocols like EAP-TLS, EAP-TTLS, and PEAP, as well as RADIUS's interaction with Network Access Control (NAC) solutions, are valuable additions to a professional's library.

Online training platforms and certification programs further expand the range of available RADIUS resources. Network and security certifications such as CompTIA Security+, Cisco CCNP Security, and Certified Information Systems Security Professional (CISSP) often include modules focused on RADIUS concepts, 802.1X deployments, and AAA configurations. These certifications help professionals develop a broader understanding of how RADIUS fits into enterprise security architectures and best practices for integrating RADIUS with modern identity and access management systems.

Security-focused organizations like the National Institute of Standards and Technology (NIST) also publish guidelines and frameworks relevant to RADIUS implementations. NIST Special Publication 800-53 provides controls for secure access management, many of which directly relate to RADIUS environments. Similarly, the NIST Cybersecurity Framework outlines risk management practices that align with deploying and maintaining secure AAA infrastructures. Adhering to these frameworks helps organizations comply with regulatory requirements and align their RADIUS deployments with industry-recognized security standards.

Publications from the Payment Card Industry Security Standards Council (PCI SSC) also highlight the role of RADIUS in achieving compliance with the PCI Data Security Standard (PCI DSS). For organizations operating in retail or financial sectors, RADIUS plays a key role in controlling administrative access to network devices and securing user access to cardholder data environments (CDE). PCI DSS documentation emphasizes secure authentication mechanisms, logging, and the principle of least privilege, all of which intersect with RADIUS-based access control strategies.

Webinars, blogs, and conference presentations provide ongoing education about evolving RADIUS trends and best practices. Conferences such as the RSA Conference, Black Hat, and various network security summits often feature sessions on AAA infrastructure, RADIUS vulnerabilities, and emerging technologies like Zero Trust Network Access (ZTNA) and Secure Access Service Edge (SASE), where RADIUS plays an integral role. These events help practitioners stay informed about new developments and gain insights from industry experts on optimizing and securing RADIUS deployments.

Automation and orchestration resources are also becoming increasingly relevant in modern RADIUS environments. Documentation from automation platforms like Ansible, Puppet, and Chef often includes modules and playbooks for deploying and managing RADIUS servers, updating policies, and integrating with centralized identity systems. Infrastructure-as-code practices are being applied to RADIUS configurations, enabling network teams to enforce consistency across distributed deployments and reduce manual configuration errors.

Finally, online communities and discussion forums such as Stack Overflow, Reddit's networking and sysadmin communities, and specialized network engineering groups serve as informal but highly valuable resources for troubleshooting, sharing best practices, and learning from peers. Professionals can find answers to common configuration issues, performance tuning tips, and creative solutions for integrating RADIUS with diverse environments and services.

By leveraging this extensive array of references and resources, network administrators and security professionals can design RADIUS deployments that meet the demands of modern enterprise and service provider environments. Access to authoritative documentation, community expertise, and industry-recognized frameworks enables teams to deploy RADIUS in a way that ensures security, scalability, and operational efficiency while staying aligned with evolving network access control trends and compliance obligations.